This book is based on the many experiences I have encountered in my life that has made me the person I am today. My faith in God sustains me, and I hope to share it with others. Married at an early age, I have three daughters. I was fleeing for my life from the excessive beatings inflicted on me by my husband. There is healing and forgiveness. The Bible tells us, "For if we forgive men their trespasses, your heavenly Father will also forgive you" (Matthew 6:14, KJV). I came to the United States of America for rescue and to seek a better life. My children are all married now and have their own lives to live.

A *Stamp*
OF APPROVAL

Keling Moseley Stewart

ISBN 978-1-68526-737-7 (Paperback)
ISBN 978-1-68526-738-4 (Digital)

Covenant Books
11661 Hwy 707
Murrells Inlet, SC 29576
www.covenantbooks.com

Introduction

I would like to introduce you to my good friend. His name is Jesus Christ, Son of the living God.

I accepted Jesus more than thirty years ago at a Sunday evening worship service when I was at my wit's end. With tears streaming down my checks, I surrendered my life to Jesus.

I have found this out so many times and on so many occasions, through many roadblocks, trials, and fears, not knowing who to turn to or where to run. When I call on Jesus, He is always there. He is everyone's friend. You have to believe and trust Him.

Acknowledgement

T hanks to God and the Father of our Lord Jesus Christ and the divine Counselor, the Holy Spirit, for allowing me this opportunity to express myself in writing this book. I would like to thank my children for the headaches and heartaches they have given me. I would like to thank my daughter, Sonia, and her friends. To Claire, I thank you for purchasing a tire for my car when I needed one. To Mrs. Kennedy, thank you for all you have done for this family, also for the television set which you allowed me to keep for as long as I could. Holly, thank you for all your help financially and otherwise. To Lynn, many thanks for all you have done for Sonia. You are awesome. To my dearest friend Cathy who always seemed to know in her heart when I was badly in need of help. Erica, we are grateful to you for your help and friendship. Last but not the least, my dear friend Millie, you are a wonderful friend. And to the many friends that have helped us along the way, I thank you all. May God bless you.

Chapter 1

When I left my husband with my three children—aged eleven, ten, and seven, I had no idea where I was going to spend the night wearing only an undergarment and a bra. I was able to get the keys to my car and drove away to a friend's home for rescue. My husband came home from work one evening while I was about to shower before I take the children for a ride. He approached me and said, "I want a divorce, and you must say yes."

I said, "If you want a divorce, go ahead and file for it because if you remember, when I left you the last time, I had asked for a divorce, and you begged me to come back and give you another chance, which I did. Now I am back and trying to settle down, you want a divorce." I walked to the bathroom and started to undress. Suddenly, I felt a blow to my head and my entire body. I screamed, but no one could hear me because it all took place in the master's bedroom. I managed to escape and run down the passageway, but my husband caught hold of me by the hair, and I felt like a football. He kicked me, stomped on me, and did everything he could do to disable me. I kept screaming until the girls, who were outside riding their bicycles, came rushing in. They were all screaming and pleading with my husband to stop, but it was no use. Then my oldest daughter struck him with an object, and he moved away to catch her. She ran swifter than a horse, and I was able to get away and run outside half naked.

The girls and I had a plan. We gathered rocks, and while I started from the front throwing the rocks, they were able to get inside to retrieve the keys to my car, my pocketbook, and my vanity carrier where I kept all my personal papers, passport, birth papers, etc. and got in the car and drove away. My oldest daughter took off her blouse and put it around my shoulder. She stayed slumped in the back seat until we reached a friend's home.

One of those times was one too many. I remembered, after an incident, I waited until he was asleep, and I melted a large can of lard (Crisco) to throw on him. Just as I was headed to the bedroom, a hand held me back. I heard a voice speak to me; I know it was the Holy Spirit. The Bible tells us in Proverbs 1:23, "I will make known my words unto you" (KJV). I quickly returned the can and hid it in the cupboard. My intentions were to throw it in his face, especially his eyes and ears, but thank God for keeping me from making that mistake.

Emily was a friend of the family for many years. When I left home the first and second time, each time she encouraged me to reconcile for the girls' sake just as my mother did; but this time was different. There was no turning back. I said I would rather beg bread on the streets than return to that house. Emily's marriage was not very stable either, yet her husband has never laid hands on her. She had two grown sons.

When we arrived at my friend's house, Susan got out of the car and went into the house and asked to borrow a dress for me to put on. After I got into the house, I explained everything to her and asked if I could stay there for the night. The next morning, I was too embarrassed to see a doctor or go to the hospital as suggested. However, I did have a doctor who made house calls. He asked if I wanted to press charges, which I did not. I thought it was a waste of time since the law never interferes with abuse cases unless death occurs.

While waiting for the doctor to examine me, I sat thinking, *Why did I ever agree to take my children and move back into the house with my husband? I was doing so well on my own.* I had obtained a loan from the bank where I worked for over eight years and had set up house for the girls and myself. We were happy and contented. We took short trips together, and everything was under control. Then one day, I had a visit from my husband. He said he wanted to see the girls. (The court ordered.) I had taken him to court for child maintenance, and the court awarded $7.56 per week for each child.

This was an insult to mothers, but I was making a decent salary. My husband said he was very sorry for all the bad things he had done to me over a period of time and promised that if I return, he would be a faithful husband and a better father. I told him I was not sure, but I would discuss it with the girls. Like a person with no sense, I found myself moving back to the house. It was a beautiful house set on top of a hill with a sundeck on the roof. The girls did not seem to regret the move and began their lives all over again.

The doctor came and examined me. After answering a few questions, he asked again if I wanted to press charges. (Like a fool, I said no.) He gave me a shot and some tablets, and he left. I realized that when you are in distress, you call on God. I stayed with Emily for two nights since her husband was away, but he was due to return that weekend. She said she could not accommodate the girls and me after the second night. I said, "I understood the situation."

I needed some clothes from the house, so I went to the police station for help. My husband, an ex-police officer, seemed to know everyone in town, and everyone was his friend. I asked for an officer to accompany me to the house to get my clothes. When we arrived at the house, the officer rang the doorbell, and my husband, apparently knowing why we were there, came to the door with a suitcase and threw it on the steps in front of the officer, not allowing me to go into the house to get my things. We left. I prayed, "Lord, why do I have to go through this shame more than once. Please help me." The Bible tells us in Isaiah 41:13, "I the Lord thy God will hold thy right hand, saying unto thee, Fear not; I will help thee" (KJV). I remember asking the Lord that if He would help me this last time, I would never return to that deplorable situation under any circumstances.

I remembered a time I had to file a complaint against my husband at that same police station. It happened after I returned from a shopping trip for the family in Florida. I had asked my husband to accompany me on the trip. In fact, I begged him, telling him it would be good for us to get away for a weekend and to let his brother, who lived with us, watch over the children. He said that was a good idea. I made reservations. I had one day vacation left before the year ended, so the following Friday would be ideal. I mentioned to a friend, Mrs.

Sandford, who visited Florida frequently, that I wanted to go there on a shopping spree. She asked if I could do a favor and call her brother, who would send a special kind of hair grease back with me.

That Thursday evening, Mrs. Sanford came by to give me the money. I invited her to come in, but she said she was in a hurry to get the children. We talked outside, then she said, "Say hello to my brother," and then she left. I was so looking forward to that time with my husband. I told him that everything had been arranged, and we would leave Friday morning and return Sunday evening. He said he couldn't go because he could not get Friday off and that I should go by myself. I told him I didn't want to go by myself, and I would not have another day off for a while and that we could leave Friday night. He then promised that he would join me on Saturday morning.

I arrived in Florida early, checked in at the hotel, and went on my shopping spree. I returned to the hotel, ordered room service, and looked forward for the next day when my husband would join me. We would dine out in style and take in some hot spots (dancing). After a shower, I settled in front of the television set. I had to call my friend's brother. The telephone rang, and it was my husband calling to say that he could not make it on Saturday as promised and I should try to enjoy myself. There was no reason for him not to join me.

Saturday was another day of shopping, and after breakfast, I set out to do more shopping. Many residents from the islands did most of their shopping in Florida because of the variety of goods and bargains. I arrived back at the hotel to find I had a visitor waiting in the lobby. Mrs. Sanford's brother, Rex, introduced himself. He had the hair grease and a few other things for his sister. After inquiring about my shopping, he asked if he could invite my family and me to have dinner with his family. I told him that unfortunately, my husband had planned to arrive today, but something had come up. Rex suggested that instead of staying all by myself in the hotel, he invited me to have dinner with his family. After dinner, the family decided to take me to the dog track in Hialeah, Florida, and after a few bets and losses, they drove me back to the hotel.

I arrived home that Sunday evening. Shortly after, Mrs. Sanford pulled in the driveway. She was taking the children out for a drive and thought she would stop by to see if I had arrived and to pick up the package. "How was the trip?" she asked.

"Very good," I replied. "Although it's disappointing because my dear husband promised to join me, but he had more important things to do." She asked about her brother and if he had sent the hair grease. I told her that he and his family were fine and that he had come to my lonely rescue and invited me to dinner and then to the dog track.

"That's my brother," she said. "He is a gentleman." I did not have the time to tell my husband about the dinner and the dog track since Mrs. Sanford came just a few minutes after I walked in the door. I had just put down my luggage, greeted my husband, and talked with the children.

After Mrs. Sanford left, I was so anxious to show off my purchases. I opened the suitcases, and the girls were admiring their beautiful clothes on the bed. My husband was in the dining room ironing his shirts for work. He loved to press his own shirts since we had dismissed Mrs. Charlton, our housekeeper. She was wonderful. However, when we began to build our house, we needed every extra penny and could not afford any help at that time. My husband said, "I heard you telling Mrs. Sanford that you called her brother and what a wonderful time you had with him. I heard everything."

I told him I had wished he were there to meet them and to make friends with those nice people. He replied, "Why should I stop you from your rendezvous? You probably see him whenever you are in Florida."

Jokingly, I told him he was jealous. "You're damned right I am," he answered.

I told him that there was absolutely no reason to be jealous. "I just made friends, that's all. I just had a pleasant evening with Mrs. Sanford's brother and his family. They are very nice people. You should have seen their house. It was beautiful and very large, a lovely family," I said.

"You did not tell me you were going to see Mrs. Sanford's brother in Florida," he replied.

I said, "It must have slipped my mind. After all, we both were expected to be in Florida, and you would have had the opportunity to meet her brother when he came to deliver the package. I did not think it was a big deal. All I had to do was call and ask him to bring over something for his sister."

He said, "He could be your sweetheart. I know all about your men."

I was about to fix dinner when he called me into the bedroom. He pulled me inside and locked the door. That was when all hell broke loose. He was like a madman. I thought he was going to kill me. I was being beaten so bad. My brother-in-law stayed in the living room and did not lift a finger to come to my rescue. I was all bloodied up and so was the clothing that I had just bought. The next day, I summoned my doctor, and after examining me, he said, "My advice to you is you have two choices—either you leave your cruel husband or stay until death."

I packed a few things for the girls and myself and went to my brother's house. Sonny was the oldest of five siblings, but only the both of us survived. The others died at an early age. Things looked gloomy for me. I had no one else to turn to, and the girls were still very young. They could not understand what was going on. Neither could I, but I did know I was not leaving my children behind. Wherever I went, they would go. All I know is that I was a faithful wife to my husband, but he could not believe that a woman could ever stay faithful to her husband. There was an old saying "Husbands blame their wives being unfaithful when in fact they are guilty of their own unfaithful act."

I had to find a place for me and my children to stay since Emily's husband was coming home that evening. I did not think for a moment that he would have objected to me staying just a couple of days, but I knew that space was very limited. Yvonne was a good friend of mine who lived in a small wooden house with her mother and a younger brother and was willing to let me stay for as long as I wanted until I found a place of my own. They were angels I believe that God had put in my path. With the help of a few acquaintances, I was able to find a back room in someone's home with the use of their kitchen and utilities. The girls and I made the best out of a bad situation. I lived with Mrs. Armbrister for three months until I found a place to rent. If I did not have a personal relation with Jesus then, I found one with the Father and Son. God became the head of my life. I learned to depend on the written word in the Bible, and I believe that after I had given over everything to the Lord Jesus that things took a turn for the better.

At the bank where I worked, the managers knew of my situation and told me I could take some time off to find a place. I found a two-bedroom furnished house, but the rent was more than I could afford. There was no electricity when we moved in that weekend, so we used candles. I returned to work that next week, and things were normal again. A friend who expressed concern over the situation found an evening job for me. The job required me to be there from 6:30 p.m. until 11:00 p.m. I had to drive several miles back and forth, which was scary, but I knew that God promised to protect me. I dreaded leaving the children all alone while I tried to make ends meet, but at the same time, I had no choice. I remember I would go into the kitchen at work and steal sugar, cocoa powder, tea bags, and milk so my children would get a cup of milk before going to bed. I did not get any support from my husband except the $7.56 weekly the court had awarded for each child. They would not sleep until I pulled the car into the driveway. My parents' concern grew, and the letters I received from them were encouraging. I prayed for guidance and direction. I made reservations to take the children to my parents.

Chapter 2

My parents lived a middle-class comical life. Alfred, my dad, was a builder and contractor, and my mother never worked a day in her life, but she played nursemaid to my dad. My dad could not get a glass of water for himself if it was to save his life. He would call to my mother, "Marlene, please get me a glass of water." She would say, "I am busy. Could you get up and get the water? After all, you are not an invalid." "No, I'll wait," he said. Mom would then leave whatever she was doing and get the water for him.

We arrived home safely on Pan American Airlines at Piarco International Airport. After clearing customs, we were driven home. It was so nice to be among family once again as everyone tried to make us happy and comfortable. We were entertained, pampered, and treated to lots of West Indian dishes by friends and neighbors. The time came when I had to part from my three girls. Parting was a bitter sorrow. I assured my children that it would not be forever. I promised to visit again on Christmas. I returned to the island and rented a room from an elderly woman whose husband left her and moved to another island to live with someone else. Perhaps it was because she had a mean streak. One good thing that came out from having to leave the children with my parents was the fact that I did not have to deal with that obsessed, over-jealous husband. I was free to travel and enjoy my life.

Vacation time came, and I had decided to visit Mexico. I arrived in Mexico City with my traveler's checks, some pesos, and a Spanish dictionary. I had taken languages in high school and understood a little Spanish just enough to ask questions with the help of the book. On my way to the hotel, I was very impressed by what I saw—beautiful flowers lined the sidewalks. I knew I would have a nice vacation.

The taxi driver was so pleasant. He spoke English when I asked him to recommend a nice hotel downtown. He took me to a very nice hotel in Mexico City. He also accompanied me to the front desk. The room was beautiful. The driver came back the next day to see if I was okay. The second day of my two-week vacation was a half-day tour to points of interest, a visit to the Pyramids, and back to the hotel. Day three was even more exciting. Upon returning, I decided to stop at the front desk to inquire how best I could travel to Acapulco, which was to be my second leg of the trip. I was discouraged by the amount of money I had to pay for a taxi to Acapulco. I had no idea it was so far. I did not do my homework before arriving, so I decided to return to the room and pray for God's direction. The Bible tells us in Isaiah 45:2, "I will go before thee, and make the crooked places straight."

On the fourth day, I had no idea what to do with the rest of the vacation. My thoughts were to either stay in the city for the duration of my trip or try to get a flight out to Miami and spend the rest of the time there. That evening, I went to the front desk to change some pesos back to dollars. While I was standing at the front desk, a gentleman, who also was at the desk seeking information, came up to me and asked kindly, "Why are you changing your pesos for dollars?" We introduced ourselves, and before I knew it, we were sitting in the lobby chatting away. I told him I had planned to visit Acapulco but could not get a tour or bus to take me there. I had no idea it was so far, so I was debating whether I should stay or return to Miami if I could get a flight out. He said that he and his friends were driving to Acapulco in the morning and asked me if I would like to join them. He then called his friends in the room and said that he was bringing a visitor to meet them. Thelma and her husband, along with her cousin Carol and a friend of the family from New York, said that they visited Mexico every year for their vacation.

After introductions, we were drinking sodas and snacks. I told them I was returning to Miami because I wanted to go to Acapulco, but there were no tours. Carol asked, "Would you like us to adopt you for the remainder of your vacation?" That night, we all got dressed, met in the lobby, and went out to dine at a fine dining restaurant, where movie stars ate on wooden plates then they signed the plates, and they were hung up on the walls of the restaurant. Pretty impressive! We drove back to the hotel lounge and had a few drinks and danced until around 2:00 a.m. We said good night with the promise they would make a wake-up call to me at around 5:00 a.m. so we could be on the road by 6:00 a.m. There were two Cadillacs, CB's, walkie-talkies, and snacks for the journey stopping off for breakfast. I wanted to pay, but they would not have it. They insisted that they had adopted me for the remainder of the trip; therefore, all expenses from here out were on them.

The streets were very narrow that looking down at the sides seemed dangerous. There were signs that read *burro crossing*, and you should not drive at night because there were no streetlights; therefore, we had to get to a village before dark and check in at a hotel. Dining at night was something to look forward to. The Mariachi bands played such sweet music, and the dinner was superb. We visited Taxco and bought silver souvenirs and visited Guadalajara and Acapulco and took a cruise on a yacht to Jalapa. After three days of fun with my new-found friends, it was time for me to return to the city to catch my plane. Since they were not ready to leave, they purchased a plane ticket for me to fly from Acapulco to Mexico City.

After my husband heard that I had taken the children to my parents, he stopped paying the small amount of money ordered by the court, which in fact did not hinder or hurt me or my plans. I had my mother hire someone to help her care for the children, and I prayed for December when I could visit for Christmas.

The manager at the bank where I worked for over eight years was very sympathetic, kind, and generous. "Mr. Young, could I see you for a moment in your office at around 3:00 p.m.?" "Yes. 3:00 p.m. is fine." "Are you sure three thousand dollars would be enough?" "Yes, sir, that is all I need to borrow."

Finally, the day arrived when I boarded Eastern Airlines headed for home to see my children with a stop first to Florida. I checked into a hotel and planned to spend two days to do some shopping before heading home. A friend who was already in Florida visiting with relatives invited me to join her and her friends on a night tour to Miami Beach, and it was a delightful treat. We visited a club where the dancers wore little or no clothes on their bodies while they wig-gled to the rhythm of the band. It was about 3:00 a.m. when we arrived at a restaurant for something to eat. The next day, my flight took off at 11:00 a.m. I arrived at Piarco International Airport at 6:00 p.m. The entire family was there to greet me with tears of joy streaming down their faces. I had lots of surprises for them.

The next day, I took my dad on a shopping spree. This was to be a surprise present for the girls. The Baldwin piano was to be deliv-ered the day before Christmas. Mom was cooking and baking up a storm on her new stove and oven, and Dad had the job of taking the children somewhere before their Christmas gift arrived. Christmas Eve night was very exciting. We decorated a tree branch, put up new draperies, the kids were banging on the piano, and I was overjoyed. It was the best Christmas I had spent in a long time. Before leav-ing again, I promised to have my children with me soon. After 18 months and my social life a bore, I decided to get an apartment and send for my children.

Things seemed to be working out fine. Sonia was enrolled at St. Xavier's, Sandra at St. Augustine's, and Susan at Queens. I had a busy schedule. I was able to give assistance whenever needed with school activities. It was a bright and beautiful Monday morning when I arrived at work feeling happy and thankful for the way things were moving in my direction. I was called into the boss's office. He said, "Please take a seat." I said, "Thank you, sir." My heart began to race miles a minute. Could it be that I have done something wrong just when everything was going right?

He said, "I would like to say my hat is off to you. Congratulations. You have been promoted to the position of supervisor in the Accounting Department."

"Thanks," I said. Could things get any better? The girls were growing up. I had planned to send Susan to school abroad so she could meet a better caliber of friends than the ones she was associ-ating with. Sandra was about to graduate from St. Augustine, and Sonia had a few years to go. I know, if God is for you, who can be against you. I performed my duties, and my employers were satisfied.

I was having lunch at my desk trying to balance the previous day's work when I was called to the front desk and was handed a very large envelope from a gentleman. Curious, I opened the envelope and was shocked. It was a summons to appear in court. The charges were not too clear and did not make any sense. I immediately went to my employer, and while I was discussing the summons, Brian, a coworker, came in with the same type of envelope in his hand. After reading it carefully, it appeared that my husband was claiming that Brian and I were lovers. Brian and his wife were from England and are very close friends of mine. Also, they were very nice to my children. We were best friends.

It was a policy of the company that after eight years of loyal service, you would get one month paid vacation. The check covered all expenses including my children's. I booked a cruise on the SS *Oceanic* bound for New York and then on to Toronto to take Susan to school. There she will enter business college and modeling school.

It was like a dream come true. We had taken a cruise before on the SS *Sunward*, but the SS *Oceanic* was very luxurious. My friend Penny, who had taken a cruise on the SS *Oceanic*, helped me to make reservations for the best stateroom. Finally, the moment arrived for us to go aboard. I had arranged with the maître d' to have a tray of hors d'oeuvres and champagne sent to my cabin, where I planned to entertain a few of my friends who came aboard to wish me bon voyage.

It was approximately 11:00 p.m., and the ship was about to set sail. After two nights at sea, we were in New York harbor looking at the magnificent Statue of Liberty. We had the first unpleasant experience as we rode an elevator on the ship's dock. Someone stole Susan's camera from her bag. After checking in at the hotel, we planned a number of entertaining things to do. For example, we went to Radio City Music Hall to see the Rockets, dine at the Rockefeller Center, visit the Empire State Building, Central Park, Times Square, and the World Trade Center. Our next stop was in Canada. The trip to Toronto by bus was diverted to a different route because of a bus strike. Finally, we arrived in Toronto at around 11:30 p.m.

The Lord Simcoe Hotel located in Downtown Toronto was a favorite of mine since I had stayed there once before. Registering Susan the next day in school was a delight. The school was not what I expected it to be, but I praised God for His blessings. The hospitality I received from my friends in Canada was graciously accepted.

After two weeks of fun and frolic, we left Susan and drove back to New York where we boarded the SS *Oceanic* for home. Cruising back was more fun than I had bargained for. The captain's cocktail party was the highlight along with several other parties. It was a cruise I would never forget. On that cruise, our waiters were handsome Italian men, three to be exact. Little did I know that one of them would turn out to be my son-in-law. Sometime later, on a bright sunny day while I was at work, I was told I had a visitor. To my surprise, it was one of our waiters from the ship. He came to inquire about one of my daughters and asked if he could see her before the ship left for New York that night. I arranged for the school bus to drop Sandra off near my office, and there we met. They came up to the office and sat and chatted for a while until it was time for him to leave, with the promise that he would like to see her again. After years of friendship, she visited Italy, they corresponded, and after a while, they got married.

Finally, the day arrived for my husband and I to go to court. I was not afraid because I had done nothing wrong. The charges were false, and I had the Lord Jesus on my side. However, I was furious about the charges brought against two innocent people who were my friends and the fact that my children would have to face another embarrassing moment. My lawyer said I had a very good case, and I knew we would be winners. Because I had never been to Brian's new house since he bought it, my children and I were invited to their apartment for dinner when his son was born. I had been invited to dinner after they moved into the new house but was unable to attend due to a previous commitment.

The judge proceeded, "This is a private hearing." My husband's lawyer began by saying that on the night of the fourth of May, I was seen entering Brian's home at 7:30 p.m. and stayed there all night. The truth was that night, Friday, May 4, the girls, along with the landlord, a neighbor, and myself were bailing out water from our rented townhouse until around 2:00 a.m. That morning, May 4, right after we all took our baths, apparently, the water was turned off for some reason (perhaps work was about to begin on the pipes in the area). However, one of the girls must have tried to use the bathroom sink before leaving, and after discovering that there was no water, she did not shut the pipe off. So when the water came on, there was no one home to turn off the pipe. That evening, when we arrived home, a surprise disaster awaited us. The water came down from upstairs onto the carpet below, and everything was soaked. The girls were very disappointed because we were planning to attend a church social that night. I recalled one night, a car pulled up almost in front of the house and stayed quite a while, but I was not interested to know who or what they were doing.

In court, pictures were shown to the judge of the outside of the townhouse showing my car. There was also a picture of Brian's house. The judge ruled in favor of Brian and me. The Bible tells us in Deuteronomy 3:22, "Ye shall not fear them: for the Lord your God he shall fight for you." The judge said to my husband, "You were misled by your hired detective. When people come into this court with lies and think they can get away with them, I do have the feelings to put them where they belong—behind bars. Case dismissed." My husband and his lawyer were made to look like fools. Brian and I had won the case, but I was very embarrassed. That incident was what prompted me to leave the island and my past behind.

Being away from work for such long periods during the case, I had to work very hard to get my work up-to-date. Life must go on, so I had decided to put the past behind me and continue with my life. Vacation time was fast approaching, and two of the girls were graduating from high school. I needed to take a trip again to the Caribbean before the girls went off to college. Reservations were made to fly to Florida, spend a few days to shop, and then on to the islands. We visited with my parents, then on to the island of Tobago with friends, to Barbados, and a brief stop in Venezuela. Every place we visited, the people were very friendly.

Chapter 3

Back to work and to the gossipers. But I had to pray for God's guidance. I knew how to pray, but I took things for granted when everything was going fine. Now I was back in business with the Lord. I began to teach Sunday school at my church and took part in church activities. Sitting at my desk on a lunch break, a coworker came by to have a conversation with me. Her first sentence was "Do you believe in witchcraft?" I said no, but I know that there are evil forces in the world. She continued to tell me about things she knew, and by her conversation, I knew that she spelled trouble. I began to have dreams and see visions. The Lord began to show me what was going on in the office. The Bible tells us in Jeremiah 33:4, "Call unto me, and I will answer thee, and show thee great and mighty things, which thou knowest not." Things began to occur in my job that I could not understand. We read in Psalm 70, "Make haste, O God, to deliver me; make haste to help me, O Lord." I wanted to leave the job in a hurry. My parents had decided that while I was about to make this move that they should be there to help.

The girls were happy for this new lease on life. Sonia and Sandra were eagerly looking forward to attending college, and the Lord made a way for Sonia to receive a scholarship to Georgetown University in Washington, DC.

Susan had moved out because she felt that she wanted to be on her own and decided to stay with her friends, which did hurt the family. I believed that by praying, God would send an angel to help me. My spiritual mother was that angel—a praying woman—and through her prayers, we saw many miracles begin to happen, as God directed.

Sandra got a job at a bank in West Palm Beach, Florida, while Sonia was waiting for her final papers of confirmation to college. It had been five months since Sandra lived with Louise and her two children along with Dillion and his cousin. Back home one night, I had a dream that I must go to Florida and look after my daughter. I booked a flight to West Palm Beach to see what was going on. When I arrived, I was told that Louise had checked into a hospital and no one could give me any reasons for her being there, which was none of my business since I had never met her. But the Lord works in mysterious ways for His wonders to perform. Sandra and I had a long talk the next day, and she told me that she was not comfortable because she slept on the sofa, and one night, while she was asleep, she felt someone breathing in her face, and when she opened her eyes, she saw Louise's brother bending over her as though to kiss her. That was the same night the Lord spoke to me "Go and see about your child." I also found out that Louise had made my daughter and Dillon cosign for a house she wanted to buy and told Sandra that she would have to share her bedroom with her two children.

I could not believe what I heard and immediately called the agent. After explaining to the agent who I was, I told him he must take my daughter's name off those documents or else! We were invited by the agent to dinner that night, and we graciously accepted. Louise must have heard what I had done, and I began to see results. We returned to the house. God began to work His miracles. Louise's cousin and her two children came into the room, which we were occupying, and began making nasty remarks about Sandra and her white friends. They carried on in the worst manner, and I knew that God was telling me something. I turned and asked Dillion if he knew me. He said yes. I asked, "Why are you behaving in this manner, cursing and insulting me like this?" He said, "I don't know." I knew then that he was only following the crowd. After I spoke to him, they all left and shut themselves in another room.

A friend of Sandra who worked at the same bank came by to take us for a ride, and we told her about the situation. I told her I could not leave Sandra in that house, and she said she would help. The next day, we packed to leave for a motel not too far away when

Gay called and said that she spoke with a friend who had a very nice room with a hot plate and a refrigerator. Before moving from the house, we discovered that some charms from Sandra's gold bracelet, a gift I had given her for her high school graduation, were missing. We decided it was not worth mentioning. They could keep them and pawn them if they were so desperate. I returned home leaving Sandra in a better situation as she continued working at the bank.

Chapter 4

Back home on the island, my family and I were looking at the television in the living room of the furnished apartment when Sonia said she thought she saw a flash of light from a tree across the street. I told her that it was probably the lightning. She said, "Mom, I don't think it was lightning," and the light flashed again. This time, I went out onto the patio, and to my amazement, I saw a man jumping down from a tree with a camera in his hand. He fell to the ground but immediately scrambled to his feet, and he picked up his camera and ran.

The next day, my lawyer called to tell me that he heard my husband was appealing the case and that my husband's lawyer said that his client had new evidence. Then I remembered the judge saying "What we have here are pictures of where the defendants live, but I haven't seen either one of the defendants in these pictures." That was when the judge decided to throw out the case. I told my lawyer about the man in the tree that fell with his camera while trying to take pictures of the inside of the apartment at around 9:00 p.m. My lawyer then concluded that it was an ignorant move on my husband's part and asked me if I wanted to go through that ordeal again. That hastened my decision to move up the time of my departure. I knew that God would give me the direction I needed for this big task.

The next day, I placed an advertisement in the daily papers. Most of the items were sold and waiting to be picked up the day before my departure, except for two carpets, my car, and a few miscellaneous items. With less than one month to go, I put up a "For Sale" sign on my car, and every evening, I would drive around the beaches and places where lots of people were. It was a beautiful Saturday evening when I decided to take the girls for a ride to the beach. My parents were enjoying the walk along the beach, and Sonia and I sat outside of the car at the side of the beach, and I said, "Dear Lord, please send a buyer for my car, someone who could pay what I am asking." I did not tell anyone on the job of my plans because I still owed for the car and did not want anyone or anything to prevent me from making my move. Also, I did not want to mention it for fear that my husband would know of my whereabouts. I called my car the Rolls Royce because it was beautiful like a Rolls Royce.

One afternoon at the beach, we had taken a barrel of fried chicken and sodas and were about to have a feast when two gentlemen came to the car window and said, "I see this car is for sale. How much are you asking?"

I quoted the price and one of them said, "Is this your final offer? It's a good-looking car, and I am interested." He asked for my telephone number. After we returned home that night, the telephone rang. The person on the other end said, "I am the person who is interested in the car. Would you keep it for my son? I will have the money in three days." I suggested that he bring a deposit the next day, and in three days, the balance would be expected. God answers prayers. The Bible tells us in Jeremiah 29:12, "Call upon me, and ye shall go and pray unto me, and I will hearken unto you."

As time drew near, I told Penny and Freddie, two of my closest friends, about my plans and destination, and then I gave one week's notice on my job. They asked about the loan, and I told them that I would try to repay it, but I could not stay on the island any longer. Sonia had left a week earlier and joined her sister who was already there and working. Finally, the morning arrived. My parents, Susan, Pepe my cat, and I boarded an Eastern Airline for Florida. There we joined the others.

I had no idea where the Lord was leading me after I arrived in Florida. What I did know was that my destination was in God's hand. The Bible tells us in Proverbs 3: 5–6, "Trust in the Lord with all thine heart; and lean not unto thine own understanding. In all thy ways acknowledge him, and He shall direct thy paths." With the money I obtained from selling my belongings, I arrived in West Palm Beach where Sandra had rented a room at a motel just across the street from her job with my visiting parents, my two daughters, and a cat. God had a plan ahead for us. That I knew. Sandra needed a car before we arrived, and God had put a gentleman, a perfect stranger, who was a friend of a friend, to sign for her to get the car. She, along with her friend, came to the airport to greet us. When we arrived at the motel, we prayed and thanked God for our new beginning. The Bible tells us in Numbers 15:41, "I am the Lord your God which brought you out of the land."

The one-bedroom unit was very uncomfortable, especially when we had to cook. One evening, when Sandra went to pay the rent, which she paid weekly, the manager told her that we could move upstairs to a suite with a kitchen, and she would only have to pay for an extra bed at the cost of thirty-six dollars a day. One Sunday night, we were in the hotel room playing games and laughing when suddenly, my mother fainted, and instantly, she was white as a sheet. We were so scared. There we were in a motel room with only the money I had set aside for the college entrance fee, and now I had to watch my mother in this condition. Then we all began to pray. We prayed so hard that I actually felt the presence of the Lord in the room. Not only did I feel His presence, but I saw a light inside the room at the entrance of the door, and suddenly, my whole body trembled. When I looked at my mother, she was back to normal. The Bible tells us in Psalm 22:5, "They cried unto thee (God); and were delivered; they trusted in thee, and were not confounded." Before we began to pray, Susan had called the paramedic. They came and examined my mother and said that her blood level was below normal, which we all knew was because of the lack of proper food.

The next day, I took the car and found a pawnshop. I pawned everything I could think off, from my wedding band to gold bracelets, binoculars, etc. It felt good to shop at the grocery store and to shop for some clothes for the college trip. Mom and dad left for their home, and Sonia had two weeks left before registering at Georgetown University in Washington, DC. It was sad to see my parents leave knowing it would be quite some time before I would see them again.

It was time for Sonia to leave for college. I had planned to use the car to drive to Washington. I met with my spiritual mother who was in Florida at the same time, and she asked Dillion if he would like to accompany me to Washington, DC. I met Dillion after I returned to Florida and was surprised how changed he was and had become a good friend to Sandra. The gold charms were returned except the horseshoe. Dillion was working at a fast-food restaurant and had just quit. He offered to drive along with Diana. We loaded the car with some food and drinks not knowing anything about the journey, but we were off to Washington, DC, with a prayer. The Bible tells us in Isaiah 41:10, "Fear thou not; for I am with thee; be not dismayed; for I am thy God. I will strengthen thee; yea I will help thee, yea, I will uphold thee with the right hand of my righteousness." The weather was beautiful along the way. We sang songs and tried to make each other happy. We made an overnight stop in North Carolina.

Chapter 5

When we arrived in Washington, DC, the weather was beautiful, but we had no idea where we were and felt lost going around in circles. Finally, we asked the first policeman we saw who directed us to a motel in Rosslyn. After a shower and dinner, we drove by the Whitehouse, the monument, and some other places of interest. The next day, we drove Sonia to Georgetown University campus for registration, helped her to her dorm, and returned to the motel. The following day, we decided to venture out a little further and went sightseeing, but we could not find our way back to the motel. I began to cry and pray at the same time. We pulled alongside the road on the shoulder and stopped a passing taxi. The driver told us to follow him. We discovered that the motel was just around the corner. Sunday morning, we visited Sonia, said our goodbyes, and drove back to West Palm Beach.

The days went by. I had no job, and only Sandra was working. With her good heart, she looked at the situation with hope. One evening, she came and announced that she had an interview with a large department store for an evening job. I asked if she did not think that the day job and evening job would be too much for her. At that point, I felt hopeless, but I continued to leave things in the Lord's hands. As she went for her interview, I went on my knees and prayed, "Dear God, please tell me what to do. I cannot find a job, and the strain is on my daughter. God, I will wait for your answer. Thank you." After a couple of days, I knew my prayers were heard because I made the decision to move to Washington. I told the girls of my decision and how I believed that the Lord was directing me to do so. Sandra got the evening job at the store and was able to credit some clothing for Sonia. I purchased a trench coat, boots, sweaters, and other personal items.

What little money remained had just about gone, and I did not know where I would find money to purchase the bus tickets to take us to Washington, DC. The remaining furniture and accessories that I did not sell, I left in the care of a friend to sell them for me. Martha had said that she wanted the remainder of the furniture and other stuff, and Thelma would bring the money upon arrival in Florida at the set date. When Thelma did not call, I decided to pay a visit to the hotel where she was staying. When I arrived, she looked me in the eye and said, "I don't want to see you." I asked what was going on. "I thought you were my friend. How could you ask me to leave?" "Well, I am not your friend anymore. Go away." I got in the car, and I remembered talking to God as loud as I could with tears streaming down my face. I knew that God had a hand in all of my affairs. He is my source. He is my friend. I felt directed by the Lord to stop and purchase a "For Sale" sign, and I placed it in the car and drove around for a while then back to the motel.

The next day, a gentleman came to see the car, but he did not want to pay the price; so I kept on praying for a miracle. Two days had passed, and on the third day, an elderly gentleman came by and wanted to buy the car for his wife and was willing to pay the price. They test drove the car and said that it was in excellent condition. He asked how soon we could finalize the sale. That night, Sandra, Susan, and I got together and prayed like we had never prayed before. We knew that the bank held the papers to the car, so we could not sell it; yet we were desperate and needed a miracle. The Bible tells us in Psalm 40:17, "But I am poor and needy, yet the Lord thinketh upon me: thou art my help and my deliverer; make no tarrying, O my God."

I told Mr. Waters that it would take about three to four weeks before the papers could be turned over to him. "Dear God, please perform this miracle for me."

Mr. Waters said, "I'll tell you what I will do. I will give you the money and take the car, and I expect the papers in four weeks' time."

Sandra said, "Sure, that will be fine with me," and he drove off with the car. At around ten o'clock that same night, Mr. Waters came back. Sandra went out and spoke with him while Susan and I stayed on our knees praying.

Mr. Waters said, "I am not sure I am doing the right thing. Where do you work?" She assured him that the bank would not hesitate to prosecute her if anything went wrong. He took the bank's address and left. That night, Susan and I packed all our belongings and were ready to leave the next morning by bus for Washington, DC.

Thursday morning came as we were getting dressed to leave for the bus station. Mr. Waters paid another visit. Sandra greeted him outside while Susan and I began to pray as hard as we could. "Please God, don't let Mr. Waters ask for his money back." Mr. Waters left as Sandra assured him that he had nothing to fear. We kissed and hugged and said goodbye to Sandra and Pepe (the cat). We called a taxi and headed to the Greyhound bus station with a large trunk, two suitcases, and two boxes. We arrived in Washington, DC, at around 9 o'clock Friday morning, depending solely on the Lord for direction. The taxi driver was very helpful in finding us a motel at a reasonable rate in Rosslyn, Virginia. After settling down, showering, and having breakfast, we bought the Washington Post and began a job search. On Saturday, we took a cab to Arlington Towers Apartment in Virginia, then we took the metro train to the YWCA in the District of Columbia in search of living accommodations and had lunch at an Italian restaurant. We were walking around Washington, DC, when we came upon a very nice hotel—a small, clean, and neat place and the rate was very reasonable for a suite. On Sunday, we checked into the hotel and then paid a visit to Sonia.

We had to find a job soon as we promised Sandra to have the money for Mr. Waters before the fourth week. We knew for a fact that he could not keep the car since the bank had the papers. God had sent a miracle whereby we could get to Washington, DC, before the winter and find jobs. The Sunday Washington Post had more jobs than you could imagine. Monday, we telephoned several offices and had several interviews. Susan had an interview that same day, and I had one scheduled for Tuesday. Our interviews went well, and I was told to expect a call before the weekend. I remembered on the bus saying a simple prayer. I said, "Lord, I wish I could find a job at a hotel or someplace where I could get a meal since the money we have is diminishing fast." The Bible tells us in Isaiah 45:2, "I will go before thee, and make the crooked places straight; I will break in pieces the gates of brass and cut in sunder the bars of iron."

It was around 7:30 p.m. on Tuesday, the same day I was interviewed, when the telephone rang. "This is Mr. Sarmiento. I was very impressed by your interview today. Your manners, conduct, and your attire met with my approval. How would you like to start work on Thursday at 9:00 a.m.?"

"I am very happy. Thank you, sir." I thought I would fly up to heaven and kiss God then come back down. Susan had made a friend while interviewing. That evening, her friend took her for a tour around the Washington, DC, area, and while she was away, the telephone rang, and the person on the other end was asking for Susan. I told the gentleman that I was her mother and could take a message for her. He said, "Please ask Susan to call this number anytime." When Susan arrived, she called the gentleman who insisted that she was the most suitable candidate for the position and would like her to report for work the next Monday at 8:30 a.m. The Bible tells us in Jeremiah 32:27 and 17, "Behold, I am the Lord, the God of all flesh. Is there anything too hard for me? Ah Lord God! Behold, thou hast made the heaven and the earth by thy great power and stretched out arm, and there is nothing too hard for thee."

I was welcomed to the staff by Mr. Gonzales, manager of the accounting department at the Washington International Club, DC, a very prestigious club where senators, movie stars, and many dignitaries dined, including Elizabeth Taylor and Mr. Henry Kissinger. The manager said, "We have a small office staff. As you can see, lunch is free and is served in the dining room. You are to be properly dressed at all times. No pants are allowed for women in the dining room, of course. You will be paid weekly, and overtime is required occasionally."

All the while at my desk, I thought of Susan who had nothing much to eat, as the money we had was just enough to pay the hotel for the week; but I was not going to forget God's miracle. I was asked if I wanted to work an extra hour or two overtime. That suited me fine because I was one block away from where we were staying. I could get a sandwich and drink. I accepted. Maria, the account assistant, took me into the kitchen that evening. There we had large sandwiches made to take back to our desk, and I was able to take home a sandwich for Susan, giving God thanks for that successful day. The next day, Friday, I received one day's pay. The Bible tells us in Psalm 107:8, "Oh that men would praise the Lord for His goodness, and for His wonderful works to the children of men."

On Saturday, Susan and I went to Roy Rogers for a bite to eat and to discuss about looking for a less expensive place. After telephoning several places, we asked the clerk at the front desk for recommendations. We were able to find a small furnished room with no kitchen, but the price was very reasonable, and we moved in on Monday night. The room was a bit crummy and in the back of the building, but that was all we could afford until we paid back Mr. Waters as Sandy had promised we would. We would not let her get in any trouble with the bank and with Mr. Waters. We spoke to Sandy after two weeks had passed, and she said that Mr. Waters came by to see if she had the papers from the bank. He gave her two more weeks before he would call the bank himself. I told her to call Mr. Waters to tell him that she would give him back the money in two weeks if at that time she could not get the papers. He agreed to accept. Susan had started working, and God would let me work overtime for the next two weeks. Susan came by to meet me while I was working overtime and was able to have a sandwich and soft drinks while waiting. That was dinner for both of us.

It was four weeks since arriving in Washington, DC, and we thanked God for our checks. That same day, I mailed a money order to Sandra for the full amount of money we owed Mr. Waters, leaving us with just enough to pay the rent for the week. It was a sigh of relief because Sandra was able to get the car back from Mr. Waters, and he would get his money back. That's how God works in mysterious ways. We had no money to travel to Washington to start our new life, so God put this kind gentleman in our path to lend us the money. I praised God. I continued to work overtime just about every evening and continued to get free meals during the day and sandwich and tea or sodas for Susan and me during the evenings. The food there was scrumptious. The desserts were made by great chefs, and each day, as I walked into that dining room and sat in the designated seats for the staff, I would silently thank God for His marvelous works toward my children and I. The Bible tells us in Joshua 1:9, "Be strong and of a good courage; be not afraid, neither be thou dismayed: for the Lord thy God is with thee whithersoever thou goest."

Chapter 6

It was November—our first Thanksgiving celebration in the United States. We were still in the crummy room. It was dark even with lights on and was scary looking, but we had a lot to give thanks for and wished that Sandra were with us. However, Sonia came and spent Thanksgiving with us. That morning, we woke up, got dressed, and had breakfast at the small restaurant in the building, after which we returned to the room and played a game of Monopoly and had dinner at the same restaurant.

The Saturday after Thanksgiving, we took the metro train to Maryland to look at a furnished apartment we had seen advertised in the Washington Post. The manager, Mr. Cober, spoke very nicely to us and showed us the apartments and promised that one would be available in two weeks. Sonia returned to campus, and Susan and I went back to work with new hope each day.

One Tuesday night, we went to bed early. We had no radio or TV, so we did not know what the weather would be like. The next morning, Susan said she had a feeling that it had snowed. We opened the window shade, and to our surprise, that white beautiful stuff called snow was on the ground. I was so excited at seeing real snow for the first time in my life. When I was growing up, I would look at post cards and admire the snow, and I longed to see and feel the real thing. However, we were not expecting it to snow so early, and I was not quite prepared. I had a pair of black boots that someone had given to Sandra and a suede coat. Susan, however, had her heavy coat which she bought when she was at school in Canada. We ventured into the beautiful white fluffy stuff and were thrilled to walk in it, smiling like two kids as we walked to work.

It was our last week before moving into a clean two-bedroom furnished apartment in Maryland. One evening, as we walked into the scary, crummy room, we noticed that the door was unlocked. It brought back memories of the man who tried to enter the room through the window at about 2:00 a.m. I remembered waking up to a sound by the window. I sat up nervously praying with my eyes fixed on the window. I saw a man on the outside trying to open the window. I shouted, "What the hell are you doing there?" Susan woke up and screamed. It seemed that the man was more scared than we were, and he fell from the fifth floor trying to climb down. After that night, we were afraid to enter the room. The next evening, after looking around the room, I did not want to spend another night there. We had already paid the rent before going into the room that night, and now we had no money. We took the complaint to the manager who promised a refund in the mail. That did not solve the problem since I had no intentions of staying in the room that night.

Susan and I had made the acquaintance of one of the desk clerks at the hotel where we lived before moving into the crummy room. We were able to find some change, and Susan made a call to the hotel while I sat in silent prayer. Susan explained the situation to Tony, the desk clerk, and he agreed to take a postdated check until Friday. He also said we could take a taxi, and he would lend us the money to pay. I raised my hands up and said, "Thank you, Lord." We called for a taxi, gathered up our few belongings, and headed for the hotel. On Friday, we paid the clerk, thanked him, and went to the room to pack our things to make the move the next day to Maryland. It was about 2:00 p.m. when we taxied to the furnished apartment, and the very first thing we did after entering was to kneel in prayer and thank God. At that time, I felt that we were like the children of Israel. The Bible tells us in Exodus 13:21–22, "God had sent a pillar of cloud to guide us by day, and a pillar of fire to guide us by night."

The furnished apartment was large and spacious, beautiful and clean. It was only two weeks until Christmas. I was very happy to see Sandy and our cat Pepe who would be joining us for our first Christmas. I arranged to pay Mr. Cober a dollar per day for having the cat in the apartment. Susan and I bought lots of groceries, and someone from my office picked up a Christmas tree for me. We bought trimmings for the tree. Clean linens were given to us twice weekly. There were dishes, pots, pans, all kitchen utilities, and a huge television set. Sonia, Susan, and I met Sandy and Pepe at National Airport on Christmas Eve. With tears streaming down our cheeks, it was a happy moment. We arrived at the apartment and that was home. I baked breads and a cake, baked a ham and a chicken along with other foods for Christmas. That day, we all felt very blessed as we enjoyed the blessings from above, with the only regret that Sandy had to fly back that evening for work the next day.

While Sandy remained in Florida, God had placed friends in her path, and she was able to move out from the motel and stayed at a friend until she returned to join us in February. Plans were made for a company to send the miracle car to be delivered at my door by a specific driver. Sandy arrived in February, and after a few weeks of rest, she was ready to find a job. I picked up an application form at the office of a bank in Washington, DC, and after an interview, Sandy was offered a position as an assistant accountant. She interviewed with two banks. They both wanted her, and after one year, she accepted the position of assistant/auditor/secretary at the other bank where she was paid a better salary.

We had decided that since God had blessed us in such a mighty way, it was time to look for a larger apartment. I thought things would work out fine, but Susan had other plans. She began to act strangely, especially when it was time to pay the rent and buy groceries. It was carefully planned that we divide all expenses. The apartment was a lovely two-bedroom unit on the nineteenth floor of a high-rise building in Silver Spring, Maryland. I was looking forward to beginning my life and was looking forward to spending our second Thanksgiving together.

My daughter Susan is a very nice person, but I could not understand the other side of her. On the weekend our new furniture and carpet were due to arrive at the apartment. Susan did not come home that Friday night. She called the next morning to say that she was spending the weekend at a friend's house. She came home on Sunday night and announced her intentions of moving out on her own. I guess if I had known of her plans, I would have been more prepared. I thought, as a mother, I was doing all these for my children, that we would never have to be homeless or live in crummy motels, and that this was the beginning of a new life for all of us. I was very hurt since I had just opened a credit account to furnish the apartment, and the rent was due that week. I said to Susan, "Are you sure that this is what you want to do?" She said yes. This was our second Thanksgiving in the United States, and we certainly had so much to be thankful to God. The apartment was furnished, and there were lots of food.

Sandra wanted to attend college after graduating from high school as her sister Sonia had. But God had blessed her with a good nature and a kind heart to make sure that things got better before even considering a college education. I strongly believed that God had worked it this way because Sonia's acceptance to Georgetown University was the beginning for us all. I did, however, feel guilty because Susan and Sonia had their chances, and Sandra stood back just to help us. Susan had promised that after her education, she would help with her sisters; but things did not turn out exactly as she said. Finally, I made a decision to do something. Susan came back twice after she left and asked to return home and promised to help with the bills, and I thought she had learned her lesson and had changed. I also thought that now that Susan was back, Sandra would have her chance to go to college, But again, Susan did not keep her promise. It was the end of the month, and she played the same game on me. I was waiting for her to come home before going to the grocery store. The cupboard was empty, but she did not come home. She called at around 11:00 p.m. to tell me that she was going to spend the night at a friend and would be home early the next morning.

The next morning, when she arrived home, she said nothing about the rent or groceries, so I asked, "Why didn't you bring the money home and then go out for the weekend or the night?"

She shouted out, "I don't have the money. I spent it."

I said, "Well, what should I do about your share of the expenses?"

She said, "I will bring it home on Monday."

I went to the grocery store and picked up a few items until Monday when I thought I would get the money from her. But when I came home from work, I noticed some of her clothes were missing, and no money was left. She called that night to say that the reason she did not leave the money was that she had loaned it to a friend until Friday, and she would bring it on Friday night. She did not leave the keys, but it seemed that while I was at work, she would go to the apartment before anyone arrived, eat whatever she could find, and leave.

I decided to catch her in the act. I asked to leave work early, citing that I was not feeling well and left at 2:00 p.m. When I arrived home, she was already there and was getting dressed. I asked her for the keys to the apartment, and she left without saying anything about the money. I did not see her until Sunday night at around 11:00 p.m. When she knocked on the door, I opened the door, she came inside, I asked her about the expense money, and she said that she did not have the money. I told her she could not stay that night and asked her to leave. But it was after 11:00 p.m. I said, "I am aware of the time, but I am sure you can call on your friends. They will come and get you as you have said many times that you have many friends to stay with if you moved from home." I was hurting, having to go to court occasionally because of late rent. The next thing I knew, she went off to North Carolina and got married. I saw the gentleman when he came to help her move out of the apartment, but I was never introduced to him nor knew of his family. Susan almost broke my heart when she came to my job to tell me that she was going to get married over the weekend and left. I thought I would have a heart attack, but the Lord took care of me. The Bible tells us in Isaiah 41:10, "Fear not, for I am with thee, I will strengthen thee, I will help thee, yea, I will uphold with the right hand of my righteousness."

Life must go on, so I decided to help Sandra. I moved into a one-bedroom apartment. Sandra and I boarded a plane for Long Beach, California, to enroll her in college. I was happy to see that day when her dreams would come true. Returning home after five days in Long Beach, it was back to my lonely apartment.

Chapter 7

D illion and I became friends again, and I helped him to find an apartment in the area not too far from where I lived. Then he lost his job and was seeking employment. I had a dream that the landlord had put his belongings outside because he was behind in his rent. They did evict him. I offered to share my apartment with him until he found a job. One Sunday morning, while sitting in church, he turned and asked me, "What's for dinner?" I pretended not to hear him.

After the service, he shouted out on the streets, "I hope you are cooking something I can enjoy because you do not cook enough for me to eat."

I said, "I am cooking quail, rice, and vegetables."

One would think I was his wife. He shouted, "That's all I have to eat?" All the way home, he complained about the fancy foods I liked to cook. We got to the apartment, and I fixed dinner. He said, "I do not want any quail. That would not satisfy me." He went to the kitchen and fixed some grits. Things got so tense between us that I realized a leopard could not change its spot. I remembered the Florida incident. Days went by and he was not speaking to me. Finally, I asked him to move out. He said, "I am not moving." While he was at work, I asked a friend to come and help me. We bundled up his things and placed them outside the door. That night, when he came to the door and saw that his things were outside, he tried his key; but I had the double lock on. He did not have access to that lock. A few years later, we both stood on the platform waiting for a train, and you would never know that we were almost enemies. We hugged and boarded the train, sat next to each other, chatted all the way, and exchanged telephone numbers. It was instant forgiveness.

He also showed me a picture of his soon-to-be wife, Julianne. I also attended their wedding.

The days were long, and the nights were short. I dreaded the weekends because I never seemed to have enough money to spend except for the rent and little food. I could not even see a movie or any paid events, and I had no friends to invite me out. I would find myself crying and feeling sorry for myself, but I continued to trust in the Lord. The Bible tells us in Isaiah 40:31, "But those who wait on the Lord shall renew their strength. They shall mount up with wings like eagles. They shall run and not be weary. They shall walk and not faint." My correspondence with Oral Roberts Ministries earned me an invitation to attend a healing seminar at the ORU campus in Tulsa, Oklahoma. It was my very first seminar, and I met and spoke to several people who attended every year. The lodging, food, and transportation to and from the airport was free. The only expense I had was the airfare.

At the seminar, I learned the secret of success, and that is by giving of my tithes and offering to the Lord. I immediately decided to put that into effect by taking out one-tenth of my earnings and some extra for the Lord's work. I attended three seminars, and what a wonderful time I had—the peaceful atmosphere, the clean grounds, and the prayer tower that was very tall and was located in the middle of the campus grounds. The students that remained on campus during their semester break were very helpful and courteous. The services with the various preachers, testimonies, and many other activities for the four days were a blessing from God.

The girls would soon be graduating, and I prayed for the day when they would be able to work and help themselves. It was a memorable year. I was laid off before Christmas. I remembered praying for a much-needed rest. I was seated by a window on the train to work one morning, looking out the window and up into the skies. I said, "God, I am so tired. I need a rest or a vacation." I heard a voice say to me, "November." I said *November*, and I thought to myself that maybe I would win the lottery or something, but instead I was laid off. On Christmas day, my two daughters came home for the holidays. Christmas was as usual, with a beautifully decorated fresh pine tree, lots of food, cakes, and other delicious eats. The girls returned to school, and I was alone again.

The unemployment checks took so long to process that I was behind in my rent each month. I was taken to court because of my late rent payment, but that was a standard procedure where they would ask when you are able to pay the rent and then you were given a certain time, and if you didn't pay on that certain date, you would be evicted.

After four months had passed and I felt a little better in my body, I took a job as a secretary at a law firm in the District of Columbia. The salary was not what I had hoped for, but it was a small office with two attorneys and one associate, an executive secretary, an accountant who served as a manager, a receptionist, and myself. I did not particularly like working with those attorneys, one in particular. One weekend, a friend and I had planned to go to Atlantic City on Saturday morning and returned on Sunday night. That Friday, at around 4:30 p.m., that attorney told me that he had some corrections on a document which he needed first thing on Monday morning on his desk. I would have to come in Saturday morning, but he would call to let me know what time he would be in the office. It should not take too long, he said; just a few corrections. Well so much for Atlantic City. That was a God stop.

Saturday morning, I decided that after work, I should be home by early afternoon and would prepare a delicious dinner. I took out a steak and seasoned it while waiting for the telephone to ring. I was at the office at 1:00 p.m. I waited outside in the lobby until 2:00 p.m. when the attorney came strolling in with his tennis racket and white outfit. He did not apologize for being late but said that the work would not take much time, and I should be out of the office by 5:00 to 5:30 p.m., and he left. I took one look at the document, and I cried. I actually sat down at the computer and cried. I had never seen such markings on any document in my years as a secretary. It would have been better if he had written it all over, and the fact that his handwriting was very poor, I could not understand half of it. It was past 6:00 p.m., and I was very hungry. I had no keys to the office, so I could not go out to purchase anything. I stopped and prayed. The

Bible tells us in Psalm 120:1, "In my distress I cried unto the Lord, and he heard me." The computer refused to work. It just shut down. I said, "Thank you, Lord."

Monday morning, the computer was fixed, and the document was completed and given to the attorney who told me he did not need it until that Tuesday. After six months, I took another job with a consulting firm as a secretary to the project manager. Anita was a kind and caring person, and we both worked well together. After two years with that firm, news came that the government was cutting several programs, and the office would be downsizing. Anita had planned to move to California. Working as a temporary assistant (temp) was a very good idea. I had many assignments and worked as a temp for five years. The agency now had new management and a new staff. I was not familiar with them, and they were not familiar with me. I got very little work, which was not enough to pay the bills, and decided it was time to return to full time employment.

I had several interviews with law firms and one with a small company. I did not pass the test with the law firms, which I did not care about because I hated working at law firms. The other company was not what I was looking for. The general office was nice, but the two by four room where I would have to work was very unattractive to spend eight hours a day in. I had interviewed with a department store but did not get the job. Arriving home, I listened to the messages on the answering machine. I had a long-term assignment with the temporary agency.

Chapter 8

I began to look back again on my life. I felt disappointed with the way things turned out. I remembered when Susan came to my job on a Friday evening and announced that she was leaving for North Carolina to get married. I thought I would have a heart attack. She was going to bring $100.00 to help me with that month's rent. (I ended up going to court the next week for late rent.) I was never introduced to the gentleman nor did I meet his family, but she was going to get married at his home. I always visualized my children getting married in a nice gown with all the traditional trimmings, and as the mother of the bride, I would be very proud of their accomplishments. Never in my wildest dreams did I expect this to happen. I thought she deserved better. She was fortunate to attend business school in Canada, and I had great expectations for her.

I loved my daughter, but we both could not live under the same roof. I was taken back when Susan, on the other end of the line, said, "Mom, did you tell Melissa that you won't take me back under any circumstances? Well, did you?"

"I think I mentioned something like that," I replied.

"But what kind of a mother are you to tell my friend that my husband and I can't come to live with you? Can't you wish me well?" Susan said.

I was so shocked that I was attacked and being dragged into a "you say" situation that my anger raged, so I put the telephone down. I could not imagine that my daughter would get down on me for words she herself had said to me. "Mom, I am never coming back." I heard those words from her over four times, but I still opened my door every time.

When the telephone rang the second time, I refused to answer it. Sonia spoke to Susan, I overheard Sonia ask the question "Why are you crying?" Before the accusing telephone call, I remembered telling Sandra how glad I was that Susan seemed to have gotten a grip of herself. In my heart I kept praying, *God, if only I had some money to help her to get a place of her own so she could make a fresh start.* In spite of everything, I wished I had the means to help or to send her away for a while until her life got straightened out. Because Susan did not listen to me, I asked God why I must suffer a broken heart. Must I suffer for her mistakes? I thought I had suffered enough. Am I an unfit mother? What was I supposed to do? Maybe if I had taken a lover while I was younger and did my own thing, I would get the respect I deserved. But instead, I trusted God and did everything for my girls to make sure they got their due share in this rough world. I once had the idea to take off for some part or parts unknown and try to start all over again because I felt like a failure. But I realized, I was not a failure. God did not make me to fail. I would rise above this with God's help. The question I asked was, if I had to do it all over again, would I have made this mistake? I took my three children and moved away from the hell and torment my husband had put me through, the shame he brought on my young children. Not knowing where I was going, the only thing that stayed in my mind was that God would guide me, and He kept His promise. The Bible tells us in Exodus 13:21, "He guided us like the children of Israel—a pillar of cloud by day, and a pillar of fire by night. Praise God."

In conversation, Susan had informed me that she contacted her dad and asked him for help. Not that it mattered, but I felt very disappointed. After all those years of struggle, I felt she should have told me of her intentions. I looked at my sick dad lying so helpless in the bed, and I felt at times that there was no way out. But with my Bible at my bed head and one in my bag, which I took to work, that was my source of comfort. That's how I managed to stay sane. The Lord said in Hebrews 13:5, "I will never leave you or forsake you."

I had a good job at a bank in Falls Church, Virginia, and after two years, I was one of the fourteen employees they laid off. Once again, my faith was tested. I asked God to send me millions of dollars. I would buy a house, a car, pay off bills, and not have to work again. That was several years ago. At times, I felt ashamed never having enough money to buy anything, especially when I am among others. Everyone seemed to have money except me. The Bible says in Isaiah 49:23, "I am the Lord, for they shall not be ashamed that wait on me." From a child before knowing the Bible, I felt left out from many things because I had no money. It seemed to be a big problem for me. When I was about nine years old, my brother and I went to a church picnic. My mother had prepared our lunch, and after eating, my brother left me and joined the boys to play a game of cricket. I was alone (not easy to make friends with) walking around the stadium when I saw an ice cream cart with lots of kids around it. Some were eating ice cream as they walked away, so I went for my cup and stood in line. I did not know that it cost money because I had none. Apparently, someone had paid for an order of ice cream, and I put out my cup to receive the ice cream. The salesman asked for the money. I told him I had no money, that I thought it was for free. He told me to go and bring back the money. I went off eating my ice cream and dared not pass near the cart. From that day, at an early age, I have always believed that I would have lots of money.

Some of my memories as a young girl were not always a happy time filled with drama. I had two friends—one named Dulan, who was of Indian descent, and the other named Daisy. My dad was a mason by trade and was sought after by many contractors because of what he specialized in: tiles, terrazzo, and many other masonry projects. All the houses on our street had no running water, so everyone would line up at the standpipe with their buckets to draw water. Dulan lived opposite the standpipe, so when I went to fill my bucket, I would see her, and we became good friends. She would, at times, get her bucket and help me carry two buckets instead of one. I loved Dulan. She was very pretty and had a long hair. She would come to my house, and we would sit on the steps, and I would play with her hair and take out the lice. As we grew up, our friendship grew less and less. Dulan was being groomed to marry a man who she never met; that was their custom. Daisy's brother John and my brother, Sonny, were friends in a running team, so his sister and I became friends. Whenever she visited at my home, we would sit on the floor of the two-bedroom bungalow house where I lived and play. One day, my dad was sitting in his rocking chair smoking his pipe and rocking away. He seemed to be enjoying himself. Then suddenly, he tumbled upside down and ended up on the floor. It was not funny, but we could not help laughing. Daisy could not stop from laughing. My dad got to his feet and chased Daisy out of the house and told her never to come back to his house.

My friends were animals. A goat bore a kid, and I would milk the goat and drink the milk. I also had rabbits and guinea pigs. My mother had her hens that laid eggs and hatched cute fluffy yellow chicks, which I loved to hold. Every Sunday, we would eat a fowl. My dad had hogs (pigs) in a pen, and whenever he killed one, he would call the neighbors for a share. But I grew up not having friends until I became an adult.

I was bullied, laughed at, and teased. One Monday evening, heading home from school, a friend and I were happily walking home when suddenly, three girls came up behind us and said to me, "I heard you said something about me." I ignored her, and she pulled at my hair. I slapped her hand away and started to run. I ran so close to the side of a ravine and was pushed face down inside the muddy water. Luckily, there was very little water in the ravine. My friend helped me to get out, and the girls were nowhere in sight. I knew the three sisters and where they lived. My mother was livid when she saw me. She washed the mud from my face and then I told her what had happened. We went to the girls' home and met with their mother. The mother called the girls and asked them to explain. Two of them said they did not do it, but the youngest said that the oldest sister did it. The mother apologized because I could have drowned if the ravine had more water in it. The mother told them to bring the whipping strap to her, but the girls had thrown it up in the coconut tree before we got there. That made it worse for them. She went outside and broke off about three or four pieces of thick branches. One by one, they laid across her lap and got a whipping I am sure they have never had before. The headmaster of the school heard of the incident, and after he investigated, they were expelled. I left and enrolled in a private school. Not that my parents could afford it, but they thought I would meet a different group of children, which was not always the case.

My route home from school was a passage through a small track with bushes on both sides. A certain group would walk by me and call me names, and they pulled at my clothes. I remember trying to get away from them and one of my shoes fell off. I went home with only a shoe. I was afraid to tell my parents. The next day, I wore a different pair of shoes (my Sunday's best), and the kids took my shoe and ran around the school showing everyone that my shoe had a big hole on the bottom and that it was covered with a piece of cardboard. I was very embarrassed, and the teachers did nothing. I told my parents what had happened. The following morning, before my mother dropped me off to school, she told me her plans. After school, I headed for the path, and so did the kids; only this time I was not afraid. What they did not expect shocked and scared the life out of them. My mother jumped from the bushes and said, "If you trouble my child again, you will see me again." They ran so fast, tumbled down, got up, and took off. It never happened again. Again, I enrolled in another school.

There were times I felt discouraged. I was feeling ill, and my nerves were raw. I would have liked to visit a doctor, but again, I had no insurance and no money. I began to feel sorry for myself. I developed a fever, but did not tell Sonia, who lived with me, because she worries too much. I felt like something was going on in my brain, so I did the only thing I knew—I prayed. "O God, please help me. I don't want to die now." It was an awful feeling, but I kept remembering my encounter with the Lord one time in my closet at around 2:00 a.m. I heard him say, *I am the God that healeth thee.*

The girls have all graduated, and I was happy. Sonia was still rooming with her college mate, and Sandra wanted to stay in California. She needed some money to pay for an apartment she would share with two other girls. The only way I could help her was to sell the car. I bought a "For Sale" sign and placed it on the miracle car and drove it to the grocery store. That evening, someone asked to purchase it. I also mentioned to the person that I was selling furniture. The next day, I sold the car and some furniture. I sent the car money to Sandra, and I kept the furniture money. I knew then that only a miracle could help me. I sold almost everything I owned except my bed. One Sunday morning, I took a large box of clothing to a flea market to sell but did not even make the amount I paid for the space, but I was determined not to give up, not to quit, to start over again and trust God.

As the New Year ushered in, I decided to make new resolutions and commitments to God—to change my pattern of living and to ask Him to have His way in my life. Through loneliness, I became closer to God and started to read a portion of my Bible every day. Things were not getting worse. It was just that it was a slow process because God's timetable is not as ours. Waiting with patience was what was required of me and believing that things would be better.

Chapter 9

God had brought me through the years amid the tears and financial depression. I decided it was time to shake off the blues. I purchased a sewing machine and some fabric to make a new wardrobe for myself and got ready to welcome home the graduates for Christmas. They were shocked to see a gaily decorated Christmas tree and a banner stretched across the wall that said "Welcome Home, Graduates," and on Christmas eve, we had a small party. We gave thanks to God for His blessings.

When I was a little girl, my mother would make beautiful dresses for me. I had no sisters, only a brother who was much older than I, and there was nothing to stop me from having a new dress every week because my mother sewed very well. On Sundays, I would go to Sunday school and was given a few pennies to put in the collection plate. I thought I was pleasing God. Every school fair, party, and event, you would see my familiar face. I even entered a dance contest and won. Life was aglow when I was out of the house but at home was something else. My parents fought just about every week. I remembered my sixteenth birthday. I had heard of words like "sweet sixteen," but my parents did not recognize such words. I did not even have a birthday cake much less a gift. I recalled sitting by the window the night before my birthday and watching the moonlight, dreaming and wishing. (I was always fascinated by the brightness of the moon. It looked magical to me.) I heard my dad ask my mother to heat some water for him to take a bath. In those days, there were no modern inside baths (at least in our case). Everything was outdoors. If you wanted to take a bath at night, you would have to use a large washtub. I heard my mother call my dad, announcing that the hot bath was ready. She also went and told him that his bath was ready.

A few minutes later, dad called me and told me to heat some water for him to get his bath. I said, "Dad, I thought mom heated the water for you." Well before I knew it, I felt a hard slap to my face, and that night, I got a beating out of this world. When my mother came to rescue me, my dad turned on her, and he beat her too. I managed to get away and ran outside. The first thought that came to my mind was that I would take every stone I could see that bright moonlit night and smash every glass window. It got his attention, and he stopped hitting my mother. That night, my mother and I slept at a neighbor's house. That was one of the many incidents in my life at home. I had to grow up quickly. I had to leave home.

My mother tried everything to help me. She enrolled me in a secretarial school. After a month, it was ended. I had known Mitchell who was sort of handsome, a dreamer, and liked to dress Hollywood style. One evening after classes, we were walking home together, and my brother saw us. My brother thought he was the king of the frontier, so he came up to Mitchell and punched him in his face, took me by the hand, and carted me off. That was not all. My dad had to do his number. I got another beating just because I was walking home with someone in a pair of pants, and that was the end of the secretarial studies. I was sent to learn to play the piano, but I had no piano to practice on. Instead of buying a piano for me, my dad bought a sewing machine for my uncle who moved out from the house without a word. I was about to rebel. I decided to continue seeing Trent because he was a nice guy. I told myself that was the last beating I would ever get. I would stay at home for my mother's sake, but no more beating, I swore. I took a job at a shirt factory and made lots of friends. My life was going my way, or so I thought. Church and Sunday school were not in the picture, but I would attend Good Friday and Easter services. I thought God would be pleased to have my presence a couple of times a year just like my dad.

Invitations would come for dances with a special band named Sel Duncan, one of the most popular bands in town and was usually by invitation only. The dress codes were mainly formal or semi-formal, occasionally barn dance clothes, no jeans. They were the kind of functions you looked forward to attending. As regular fans, my friends Elsie, Lorna, Niles, and others were often there. I was invited to a semi-formal type of function not with the usual group but with another friend who introduced me to a friend of hers. This friend was kind of handsome (turned out to be my husband), well-dressed, and he danced with good rhythm. We danced almost every number. I made an enemy with my friend just because the gentleman was her date. I introduced him to the group, and we continued to attend the best formal functions, ate at the best restaurants, and danced to the wee hours at New Year's Eve parties.

My parents approved of this latest flame, but his parents and my friends did not. They thought I could do better, but I was going to leave my father's home one way or the other. So I married the guy. His family did not attend the wedding, so who cared as long as I got out of the house and got married as my mother wanted me to do. My parents were proud that their daughter was getting married, which was a great honor to them in those days, all expenses paid.

At the birth of my first child, my husband's parents did not visit, until the christening. They showed up with their entourage and their own foods. They looked at the beautiful baby, and I heard the remark "This is not my son's baby." I thought she was too beautiful to be related to any member of his family. When I had my second child, my family and I moved out of the country.

God had a hand in all of my life. I remembered when I was a small child, I would go under my parent's house, which was built high above the ground. I would wish that someday, I could leave my homeland and go to the United States of America. I did not know that you could talk to God as I know now, but I guess God saw how innocent my request was in asking. When I grew up, I realized God does hear and answer prayers. All you have to do is ask, believe, and wait.

Chapter 10

I was unemployed again. I had been on several interviews, passed the tests, and still no calls. Lying in bed one rainy Saturday morning, reading my Bible, I heard these words clearly, *If you do not meditate on God's word, you will not be able to stand the pressure that comes against you.* I knew that it was the Holy Spirit speaking to me. I opened Psalm 37:4, and it said, "Delight thyself also in the Lord; and He shall give thee the desires of thy heart." David was in great distress, maybe he never worked in an office or in our modern-day world, but he was distressed. His life was in danger, and what did he do? He turned to God as we read in 1 Samuel 30:6. We read in Isaiah 26:3, "Thou will keep him in perfect peace whose mind is stayed on thee because he trusted in thee." Then I realized, if I would heed those words, I would not go crazy because I thought I have no husband, no friends, no job, no insurance, and no money. But I know the Lord; therefore, I would keep my eyes and mind on Him.

I was grateful for the apartment complex I shared with my youngest daughter Sonia. It had been over a year since my dad came to live with us after my mother passed away. There was no one to take care of him. When I received the news that my mother had passed away, I was shocked. My parents were preparing to come and stay with me since they were getting up in age with no one to take care of them. It was a brave gesture for me to take them under my wing when I did not have a steady job at that time. My mother had just finished sorting some things to give away to charity. That evening, while she was relaxing on the patio, she told my dad that she was not feeling well, so he walked her to the bed and laid her down. As he comforted her, she lifted her hands and pulled him to her face, kissed him, and went home to be with the Lord. My dad was in shock. "I did not get to tell her I loved her," he said. But God knew that I could not manage to care for them both, so God took my mother home, which was a blessing.

My dad arrived the next month to live with us. I recalled my younger days with my dad. They were not too pleasant. My dad apparently did not know how to show love. He was very strict. Now I have my children, I understand the importance of his strictness. He did not object to my friends or my social life, but to just one person in particular for whom I had a crush on.

I remembered being invited to a Saturday night social. I knew Mitchell would be there, but my dad made me promise not to dance with him or have anything to do with him. That was hard to do, but I promised just to go to the dance. Mitchell and I danced together and joined the crowd with laughter and fun. We had a ball. After the dance, I stepped outside only to see my dad parked with his bicycle waiting for me. He said he had stayed there all evening watching us. When I got home, I got a beating, but that did not stop me from seeing Mitchell. After all those beatings, I hated my dad. Now I had to take care of him.

Before Dad passed away, he deeded his property over to me. I took a trip to his hometown to sell the property. My dad instructed me on how I should spend the money. I purchased a condominium. Sonia, my dad, and I, along with my miniature Yorkshire Terrier (Cliff), moved in the condo in haste because I was given notice to move out of the high-rise apartment since I had a pet. A few days after I moved in, someone knocked on my door. It was a condo owner who lived below me. I was told that whenever I use the master's bathroom, it leaked down to her condo. I never had the opportunity to use that bathroom. We were contented to live there for the time being. I took care of my dad while working as a secretary to the manager at a bank. My boss was very understanding of my situation if and when I was a little late. On mornings, I would give Dad a bath, change his clothes, feed him, and fix lunch for him. I would put the lunch on a table next to the bed along with a radio, and he would stay there until I returned home on evenings. I did that for almost a year. He could no longer walk by himself. I had to take dad to an emergency clinic because he was in a lot of pain. The doctor said he had prostate cancer, which I figured out myself. The doctor gave him some pain pills and told me he would not live for long unless he had surgery. My dad said, "No surgery." He was eighty years old. He died at the age of eighty-three. After he passed away, I decided to sell the condo. The agent placed the lockbox on the door, and in three days, I had someone who was interested in purchasing it because of the interior. I had spent a few dollars on the interior, which paid off. There were four other condos up for sale in the building, but I got the sale within one week.

It was long before I met my dear friend Millie, when we both were members at a United Methodist Church, when this little incident occurred. It was at a Sunday morning service when I was scheduled to assist in serving communion. As I was about to serve, a woman sitting in the pew looked fiercely at me. Her eyes were cold, and she said, "I do not want you to serve me." She got up from her seat, walked across to the other server (a white woman), took the bread and wine from her, and returned to her seat. People stared at her in disbelief and shook their heads. I continued to serve with a smile as if that incident did not occur. I felt sorry for that person. She should have cleansed her heart before partaking of the Holy Communion. Christ Jesus died for us—blacks, whites, and all others. He paid the price for all.

After one Sunday morning service, a lady who was sitting at the back came and introduced herself to me. Her name was Millie. She said that she was one of the captains of the ladies' group in the church and asked if I would like to join her team. I was so impressed because I had attended that church for several years and was never asked to join the ladies' group. I stood there looking at this person from head to toe because she was so beautiful, well-dressed, had an angelic face and flawless skin. She spoke softly, and she had a beautiful smile. I graciously accepted the invitation. She then drove off in a beautiful, shiny black Cadillac.

I was invited to join her and her husband for dinner at their home several times. Millie was born in North Carolina, USA, and I was told that her husband was from England and lived in the Middle

East for many years. Their pen pal friendship blossomed. They got married and settled for a while in Virginia. Our friendship lasted for many years. She encouraged me to join the ABWA or the American Business Women's Association, and I looked forward to every event. We traveled to many cities for their conventions, and I would get to make new clothes. One of the conventions I was especially fond of was held at the Bonaventure, the host hotel in Los Angeles. Millie and I stayed at the Hilton. The social events were at four different hotels and in four categories—the Gatsby, Big Band, Gidget, and a Western. You were required to dress according to the category you chose. I chose the Gatsby because I loved that era. My red-fringed dress was accessorized with long white gloves and a headband with a long feather. It was held at the Biltmore Hotel. Millie chose the Big Band, and she wore a long flowing white taffeta gown. We both looked very beautiful walking through the lobby to a waiting cab that would take us to our different hotels. At the end of the functions, everyone gathered at the main hotel (Bonaventure). We took off our shoes and danced around the fountain. Truly we were having a rollicking good time. I was sad when it ended.

Many years have since passed. God is still very good to me and my daughters. On July 23, 1995, I became a citizen of the United States. What an honor and a big step for me. My friend Millie came from North Carolina to celebrate the occasion. I gave praise to God.

Once again, I was unemployed. I had planned a cruise on the Royal Caribbean to Jamaica, Cayman Islands, Haiti, and Mexico. Vicky and I traveled to Miami to join the ship *Majesty of the Seas* for a seven-day cruise, which started on New Year's Eve. After checking into our room, we got dressed for the captain's ball. It was an evening to be remembered. Almost everyone was dressed in their evening attire and ball gowns with their best jewelry on. I wore a strapless formal gown made up of a tri-colored blue sequin top attached to a blue organza skirt with bias frills and earrings. Vicki wore a beautiful heavily beaded formal gown and chandelier earrings. We were called the two divas as we welcomed the New Year in style.

Upon arrival at the Cayman Islands, the seas were rough, and the ship had to anchor out from the dock. We were taken ashore by small boats, then by cab to downtown Georgetown, the shopping area, because the water was too rough for the ship to dock at the usual docking place. I took my Louis Vuitton bag with all my documents instead of taking my small shoulder bag. Later, I thought it was stupid of me not to leave important documents in the ship's safety box (but if I did, I could not board the ship without showing some documents). I remember taking out a $5.00 bill from the bag for the cab, but when we arrived in Georgetown, I came out from the cab with my camera on my shoulder and left the bag behind. I realized that I had no bag when my friend went into a store, and I was standing at a telephone booth waiting to call a friend who lived there. (The bank where I worked had sent me to their branch in the Cayman Islands to resolve some difficulties in the accounts department, and that is where I met my friend, a former beauty queen.) Later, I learned that she was in the United Stated visiting with her children.

I panicked and rushed back across the street to look for the cab, but it was not there. Then Vicki came out from the store, and I told her what had happened. We both decided it was time to report the matter, so off we went to the dock master. I was so scared. I prayed as I had never prayed before. Many calls were made to the ship and the pier where the ship had docked. Vicki stayed at the corner where the taxis were parked, waiting to see if the taxi driver would return with the bag.

My deepest concern was how I would reenter into the United States. The bag contained my passport, driver's license, traveler's checks, and other documents, and the ship was scheduled to take off at 5:00 p.m. sharp. A certain gentleman who was helping with the calls kept saying "You will get your bag." But with all the faith I had, I was scared. I cannot explain how I felt. It was as though my spirit was saying to me to be still. The Bible tells us in Psalm 46:10, "Be still, and know that I am God. I will be exalted among the heathen. I will be exalted in the earth." It was suggested that I call the passport and immigration office to see what could be done. I spoke with a gentleman who said there was nothing he could do because all government offices and the US Embassy were closed because of the holiday.

I remember standing outside the dock master's office, and with my face toward the heaven, I shouted out, "Lord, please do not forsake me. I have no one else to help me." The Bible tells us in Hebrews 13:5, "I will never leave you, nor forsake thee." I left and walked back to where I had left Vicki. As I was crossing the street, I said a prayer. "Lord, please let whoever finds my purse be kind and compassionate. Let them return it with everything inside." I went to the corner and kept looking for Vicki and the cab. I walked back to where some other cabs were but did not recognize the taxi we had taken, so I turned back to the corner when I spotted Vicki coming toward me with the bag held up high. I did not wait to hear how she found it or where. I took the bag, looked inside to see if everything was there, then I knelt down in the middle of the street with everyone looking at me. I raised the bag up to heaven and gave praise to God. The Bible tells us in Isaiah 55:6, "God said to call on Him." He is closer to you than a brother.

When we returned to Miami, we were told that a storm had hit the Virginia area, and all flights were canceled. We immediately called the hotel where we had stayed before and were fortunate to obtain a room, although we were told that all rooms were filled with stranded passengers. The next day, after calling around the clock to the airport, we were able to get on the first flight that Wednesday in first class seats. I had never seen so much snow since I had been living in the United States. However, I was glad to be home when I found out that Sonia had been ill all week with the flu.

I was still unemployed, and I tried to find work unsuccessfully for one year. Sonia came through for me. She is truly a blessing. I was always impressed by her devotion and consideration to me since I was not bringing in the bread. I asked her one day about getting married. She said to me that it seemed everyone had left and that she felt she had to take care of me. She was worried that if she got married, what would become of me? I told her that God would provide for me and that she should not let my situation hinder her from having a life of her own.

The rented condo where Sonia and I lived looked beautiful. The Christmas tree with all the trimmings, the drapes, the colorful decorations, and the food, all were quite pleasing. Sonia gave me a computer for my Christmas gift. After dinner and when everything was settled, I sat alone in the living room looking at all the beauty around, and tears came to my eyes. I had always wanted to live in a single-family house or a large town house. With tears streaming down my face, I said, "God, please do not let me spend another Christmas here or in any other apartment." I thanked God in advance for answered prayer. Every weekend, I would look at the real estate housing section, and I would even drive to locations to look at houses and visualize living in one, not letting anyone know.

One Saturday, Sonia came to me and said, "Let's go and look at houses." I said okay. She picked up the real estate section, and we drove to a new development where several houses were in progress. We visited one model town house, which we both liked. Sonia went to the office and inquired about cost and down payment and others. On our way back home, she asked me what I thought about getting a town house. I was so shocked that she would ask that question. I told her that it sounded great. We arrived home, and Sonia went to the movies. I had the place all to myself. I knelt and thanked God as loud as I could. I hoped the neighbors did not hear me. I did not say anything more to Sonia about the housing situation. The next week, she came home from work and announced that she was going to get some money from her pension to make a down payment on a townhouse. Construction began with her own specifications of certain things like cabinets, backsplash, and kitchen floor tiles. We moved into the new town house in August. No one can say that God does not answer when you pray to Him. He sometimes takes longer in certain cases, and at other times, He answers right away. I didn't think my prayer that Christmas was special. I just asked and thanked Him in advance.

Thank God, I have lived to see the new millennium—the year 2000. What a blessing. Now I am recapping some of the things that took place in my life. One of them made me very disappointed. I thought I had found my knight in shining armor. My friend Millie's husband (an Englishman) gave her a birthday gift that was super. She invited three of her closest friends including myself to join the celebration. I flew to Atlanta, Georgia. We drove to Florida and stayed at a hotel to wait for the others. We then cruised to the Bahamas and back. At the hotel, I met a tall handsome gentleman who worked there. I offered him a slice of my favorite cake, which I took with me to celebrate Millie's birthday and Denise's engagement. Upon leaving the hotel after our fabulous cruise to the Bahamas, the gentleman and I exchanged addresses and telephone numbers. I received a letter from him three weeks later, to which I responded. His letters were so well written and versed. I asked him if he had been a valedictorian or if he had someone write his letters. I judged him on his words, which were intelligent, and I loved the way he expressed himself. He asked me for a picture, but while I was preparing to send him a photo, I distinctly heard a voice that say, *Do not send a picture.* But I did not listen.

Desperate for a friend, I went ahead and sent the photo, and he, in turn, sent one of himself. We corresponded for eight months. During that time, I invited him to visit Washington, DC, to see the great historic sights. He said that he could not get away at that time but would love for me to visit where he could take me to see some of the sights, enjoy some fancy restaurants, and show me a good time. After thirty years of separation from my husband, I finally got my divorce, which called for a celebration. A thought came into my mind to take a trip to the Atlantis Hotel in the Bahamas, but instead, I opted to go to Florida to visit some friends and to see this gentleman. I wrote, telling him of my plans to visit and asked him if he would be able to take time off to help me celebrate, and if he couldn't, I would go for Plan B, which was to go to the Bahamas. He called to say that the first plan was a great idea.

He wrote a letter saying that he had booked a room for himself at a very nice hotel. I told him where I was staying, just two blocks away. He agreed that we would have a good time. I was met at the airport, and my first turnoff was the way he was dressed. It was not how I expected him to look when welcoming someone who he barely knew. I decided to overlook that at the time. We stopped at a grocery store for items I needed such as strawberries, water, champagne, etc., including some flowers. I told him that I like to have flowers in my room whenever I travel. His lame excuse was "I wanted to get you some flowers, but I could not find a flower shop." On our way to my hotel, I asked if he had already checked in at his hotel. He said that he did not check in because they wanted to charge him too much, and they were trying to rip him off, so he decided that he would prefer to drive back to his home, which was about twenty minutes away. I checked in to my hotel, and we made the way to my room. I took one look at this person, and my stomach began to turn. It was as if he were a twin of the person I had first met. The outfit he was wearing turned me off.

It was dinnertime, and I was hungry. I wanted to eat in the dining room. He said, "I don't think they will allow me to enter with my jeans. I will have to change."

I asked, "Did you bring a change of clothing?"

"It's in the car," he said. He went to his car and came back with a paper bag in his hand with his clothes. "Could I use the bathroom to change?" he asked. He came out wearing a similar outfit, and he looked the same. At that time, I was thinking, *I did not want to be seen eating in a dining room with him looking that way.* There I was, well dressed, and this guy is looking like a bum.

I said, "I do not feel like eating in the dining room because I am not very hungry. Could we find a place to have a bite to eat?" We ended up at a small restaurant he raved about. We returned to my room, and I asked him to leave for twenty minutes so that I could get dressed. I changed into a beautiful black and red silk pantsuit and turned on my portable CD player with some music. I removed the hotel lamp and placed it on the table, put in a red bulb, and added a lace cloth with a vase, which I had brought from home. Flowers, chocolates, strawberries and whipped cream, and champagne and plastic goblets—all beautifully graced the table. After all, I intended to celebrate my freedom. The atmosphere and mood were very romantic. I had intended to have a nice evening and try to get to know this person who said he was very interested in me. After twenty minutes, he knocked on the door. I remembered praying silently, "Lord, I do not know this person. Please protect me."

When he entered the room, he said, "You did this for me?" I tried very hard to make the evening as pleasant as I could until it was time for him to leave, after two glasses of champagne, strawberries with whipped cream, and chocolate. My first mistake was to ask him to dance instead of waiting to see if he was going to ask. I said, "Let's dance." He was like a piece of lead. His feet did not know which way to go, so I said, "How is it that you cannot dance?"

"I never had the opportunity to learn," he said. He sat on the bed and then laid back. "I could sleep right here," he said. We began kissing as we both sat on the bed. Then suddenly, as if a hand pulled me away, I heard a voice, as clear as day, saying, *Don't. Just get up.* I immediately got to my feet and sat on the chair looking at him.

I said, "You have to leave now."

"Now?" he asked.

"Yes," I replied.

His face turned red. By the time he got to the door, it had turned brown. He opened the door, and the look he gave me was as if to say "You b…" I would never forget the look in his eyes. They were cold and had a look of disappointment. After he left, I made a dash to the bathroom and brushed my teeth until they shined and followed it with a double dose of Listerine mouthwash. Then I prayed, "Thank you, Lord, for watching over me."

The next day, the gentleman came to meet me in the lobby of my hotel with a pink camera case in his hand. I was so embarrassed that I wanted to hide from him, but then I thought that perhaps this was the trend in the Art Deco world in Florida; but we were going out to dinner that night, and I would get a proper image of him. We drove around Florida and returned to the hotel at around 5:00 p.m. Just before I got out of the car, he said, "I cannot take you out to dinner tonight because I have to work early in the morning, but we will have dinner tomorrow night." I went to my hotel room, showered, dressed, and went to the dining room for dinner. After that, I went to the bar, ordered a couple of fuzzy navels, got on the dance floor, and danced the evening away.

Saturday came, and I was getting excited about putting on my beautiful black silk evening gown with spaghetti straps for dinner and a show at the Fountainbleau Hotel. After a quick dip in the ocean, I roamed the beach and the boardwalk, returned to my room to shower and dress. Around 7:00 p.m., I got a call from this gentleman saying that it was too late for him to get there for dinner and that he was sorry. I said that was fine. He said, "I was thinking, I would come on Sunday and take you to the airport on Monday."

I told him thank you, but I had arranged for a tour and transportation to the airport. My friend Lynn picked me up from the hotel for an Easter Sunday brunch at her home with her husband and family. I had such a good time, and the conversation was quite interesting. I still wanted to give this gentleman a chance to prove himself even though I knew that nothing would come of the friendship. I arranged to meet with him in the lobby at 5:30 p.m. on Sunday. I left my friends at 5:15 p.m. and headed for the hotel. There were no messages. I changed my shoes, freshened up, went to the lobby, and stayed there until 6:00 p.m. I realized that I had been stood up again. I returned to the hotel and started to pack, then the telephone rang at around 8:00 p.m. I heard a voice say, *Do not answer the phone.* This time, I listened and did not answer. It rang again at 8:15 p.m. Around 11:00 p.m., I picked up the phone to hear the messages. I could not believe that this jerk had the nerve to say "I came by with some gifts for you, and I waited until 8:30 p.m. Have a good flight."

I arrived home safely. It had been a bad idea to go to Florida. I did not receive a call from this gentleman to see if I had arrived home safely. My thoughts were that he had planned to see me in my hotel room the night before I left and was disappointed that his plans did not work out. My angel was working around the clock for me. After three days, I wrote a nice note thanking him for the lovely time and hoped that he have a nice life. Two weeks later, the telephone would ring around the same time on evenings twice a week, but no one spoke. I knew the person was still on the line. Since I did not have caller ID at that time, I could not see the number. One evening, when the telephone rang, I picked up the phone and said, "Stop calling me, you jerk; this is harassment." I knew the person was still on the other end, so I hung up. After praying about the situation, I decided to test him out by sending some Christian literature and a booklet with the gospel of Matthew, Mark, Luke, and John with underlined verses. That did it. He called that same weekend saying, "I wanted to thank you for your findings."

I said, "Why do you keep calling and not saying a word?"

He did not answer, but instead he avoided answering the question by saying "I did not like the way we parted. I am so sorry. I was afraid you would not speak to me again."

I asked, "Why did you act so silly?"

He said, "I thought you loved me and that we would have sex, but when you told me that I had to leave the hotel, I knew you did not love me." Have you ever heard a quarry blasting? I blasted at him until you could see the stones heading in all directions.

"You thought I was visiting you to have sex? First, I was not impressed with the way you were dressed to meet me at the airport. Secondly, you failed to take me out to dinner as you had said you would. Thirdly, I don't know you any more than the man on the moon. And fourthly, you could have AIDS, or you could be a killer or a criminal."

He said, "I was scared and foolish. I did not know what made me act that way." After I had finished sandblasting him, he asked, "Could I call you sometime?"

"Sure," I said. When I heard from him, I received a Halloween card with the face of a black cat in the front. I gave a quick glance at the words (again beautiful words) ending with "love." I immediately tore the card in two and lit it with a match. I found a clipping I took from the internet that included a verse from an email and underlined what just suited him and a sticky note at the side, where I had underlined "last train from Virginia," and mailed it. I have learned my lesson through that episode. I would never spend money to travel to meet any man, interesting or not.

Chapter 11

I invited my best friend Millie to visit me in July for her birthday celebration and to see the new town house that my youngest daughter had purchased. We celebrated in style. First, we went to the Kennedy Center for dinner on the rooftop then took in a show *Titanic*. Millie loved the Kennedy Center. Whenever she visited, I tried to include going there for a show. The following evening, after a day of shopping and feeling half exhausted, we took a cruise around the Washington Harbour on the Odyssey. We had some eventful times together. I remembered when she invited me to North Carolina at the opening of her pet cemetery. I had decided that I would go straight from work that Friday evening to attend the ceremony at 9:00 a.m. on Saturday. Many interesting people were invited, and she wanted me to attend. It was my third time driving to North Carolina, and I normally travel during the daylight hours. This was an exception. I wanted to be there for my friend and her new business.

The case between Clarence Thomas and Anita Hill was a hot topic. My radio was tuned in to a Christian station, but every so often, I would listen to the case. During that time, I missed my exit and found myself driving for miles in unfamiliar territory. It was dark, and hardly any cars were passing by. I then saw a sign that read "Rocky Mountain." That was when I knew I was lost. I continued to drive, and with my eyes on the gas level, I kept on praying. I saw bright lights ahead of me at the side of the road. Someone's car had broken down, I thought. I stopped and slightly rolled down my windows, and there stood a very tall man leaning against his car. I told him where I was going. He replied, "Lady, you are way lost. You are miles from your exit and heading to the Rocky Mountains." He told me where I would find a gas station. I thanked him and drove off. Looking back, I did not see the car or any lights. After filling up with gas, I went inside to ask the manager for a map and to inquire about any hotels or motels nearby. I was so scared. I did not know what to say, so I told the manager that I was lost.

A gentleman with a British accent was standing at the counter talking with the manager. He heard me say I was lost. He asked me where I was heading. He looked at me and said, "Ma'am, you are so lost indeed. What are you going to do?" He told me how he could help. He said he was standing there for no reason because he left his wife (who also had a British accent) in the car and came in to get a Coke. Then he started talking to the manager. Perhaps he was supposed to remain there to help me. He took me to the car, and his wife came out and introduced herself when she heard of my plight. He wrote down his license number and gave it to me just in case, but he suggested I should drive as close to them as possible because they were going in that direction to attend a wedding on Saturday. I drove behind them on the dark streets for almost one hour, praying and hoping to see something familiar. Then I spotted some familiar locations.

He pulled off to the side, got out, and directed me to drive straight ahead. I knew then where I was, and I thanked him and his wife. I believe they were angels sent to help me. The Bible tells us in Psalm 91:11, "He shall give His angels charge over thee, to keep thee in all thy ways." I stopped at a restaurant at around 11:30 p.m. and called my friend to let her know that I would be there in a few minutes and then I would explain. Both she and her husband were very angry with me because they were worried. I didn't blame them, but at that time, I was not thinking straight. I was very scared. What I got out of this experience was the moment you take your eyes off the Lord Jesus, you are likely to make a wrong turn.

Needless to say, 1999 was not a bad year. I still had my health. I was working until I would soon retire. Another great thing happened that same year. In November, my daughter adopted a beautiful baby girl. She had been in the foster care system, and when we found her, she was seven months old. We were allowed to visit her at the foster home until the papers were ready. She was so attached to her foster mother that she cried whenever we were there and held on for her dear life. I would pray and ask God to give her a calm disposition and not let her miss the foster mother and not cry when we took her home. My prayers were answered. That morning when we arrived at the agency to pick her up, she did not shed a tear. We drove her home, and all she did was stare at us. When we arrived home, we took her to her beautifully-decorated room with a Noah's Ark theme and clouds in the ceiling, a dove over the door, and a rainbow against her crib. She looked around the room as if she was saying to herself, *This is home.* She adjusted quite nicely. Four years later, Sonia and her husband purchased a house and adopted a three-week old baby boy. His sister named him Nicholas, and now she has a brother to play with. They are growing up fine and are doing well in school. Val swims, plays the piano, and takes dance lessons, and sometimes plays basketball. Nicholas also takes swimming and basketball lessons and tae kwon do, a form of martial arts. He is learning to play the flute, guitar, and has his first black belt. They are now 2021 college and high school graduates.

Chapter 12

In 2008, a letter arrived in the mail with an invitation for Val to be a contestant at the National American Miss pageant for junior preteen in the state of Virginia. I had never heard of NAM. Her mother and I decided to do a little investigation. We thought it would be good for her, so I wrote back to NAM and received the necessary forms to enter the pageant.

The pageant was held at the Hyatt Hotel in Reston, Virginia. I needed to take a trial run to the hotel since I get lost easily when I am not familiar with the area. Sonia and I set out assisted by her GPS. I took notes directing us how to get to the hotel on the pageant weekend. Maggie (the name for her GPS) told her to use I-66, but instead, Sonia took the parkway. Registration began on Thursday at 2:00 p.m. Val, her brother, and I left home around 12:00 noon for the hotel using the written directions. I must have missed a sign or turned off at the wrong exit. Whatever I did was not right, and I ended up being lost. I stopped and asked several people, and each one gave me different directions.

I continued driving even though I knew I was heading in the wrong direction. I did what I normally do—I prayed. I said to the kids, "Grandy is lost, so start praying." Time was of the essence; it was around 1:30 p.m. I kept on driving with two thoughts—one to turn back and go home or turn back close to the parkway and start the route all over. These options were not suitable because my grand-daughter would be very disappointed. Somehow, I turned left to an upscale residential neighborhood. I pulled up at the side of the road, leaned my head on the wheel, and began to pray. I did not let the kids see the tears in my eyes.

I lifted my head up to see an elderly gentleman heading in my direction with his jogging clothes on. I opened the window and showed him the direction I had written down and asked if he could direct me to the Hyatt Hotel because I was lost. He tried to explain, but it was not registering in my brain. He turned and said good luck. I thanked him and turned on the engine. Just as I started to drive off, the gentleman stopped me and said, "Wait here. I will take you to the hotel. My car is just up the street." He got into his car and handed me a piece of paper with his license plate number and said, "Follow this car; that is why I am giving you the plate number." It took us about thirty minutes to get to the hotel. That is when I realized that I had strayed far from my destination. Upon arrival at the hotel, before I could get out to say thank you, he just honked his horn and drove away. The Bible tells us in Psalm 91:15, "I will bless the Lord at all times: His praise shall continually be in my mouth. Praise God."

There were sixty-one junior preteens from ages seven to nine, and their families were already at the registration. The competition was judged on poise and presentation in formal wear, personality during an interview, onstage personal introduction, and community involvement projects. Later that evening, the girls took to the stage for rehearsal. The pajama party was a hoot. The girls took their pillows, stuffed animals, and other sleep comforts. They danced until 8:00 p.m.

The following morning, the contestants were asked to introduce themselves onstage by saying their names and hometown. Then it was followed by an interview with the judges, and later in the evening came the talent competition. Contestants were able to showcase their individual interests, gain confidence, and be recognized for their talents. Val entered the stage for her talent contest wearing a beautiful red dress and played on the piano "The Woodchuck Chucks Wood."

On Saturday, the final day of the competition, each contestant, dressed in their suits, entered the judge's room for their individual interview. The aqua suit I made for Val was very well tailored and received many compliments. The highlight of the pageant was the formal wear competition, which started at 6:00 p.m. For the contestants, it was a moment alone in the spotlight, wearing the dress of their choice. When the contestants were introduced on the stage, they each were escorted by a male friend or a relative. The dresses worn by some of the contestants were very beautiful. The gown worn by Val was of a light pink satin formal with an overlay of organza on the skirt. The bodice had narrow straps and an olive-green satin bolero with a floor-length sash tied at the back with a pink rose. It was a weekend of fun. It was enjoyable to see Val socializing with girls in her age division. Val was among the twelve semifinalists out of sixty-one other contestants.

The next year, I wanted her to have another chance, so I did everything I could to get the money for the entrance fees. I took every piece of gold I could find in my jewelry box and sold them. Once again, it was time to find our way to the Hyatt hotel. With the children in the car, I headed for the road with my very own GPS (Bella). I followed Bella's instruction and arrived safely and on time at the hotel. Everything was the same. Val had two talents to perform. She entered the stage wearing a poodle skirt, shirt, and socks, and she had the audience clapping and stomping their feet while she did the Hula-Hoop swing to the tune of "Jailhouse Rock." For the second half of her talent, she wore a pink sequined jumpsuit with a matching cap and played "Jukebox Boogie" on the piano. Val won the second runner-up in the talent competition among over sixty-one other contestants.

In the evening formal wear competition, the dresses were more extravagant and breathtaking than before. Val wore a deep pink satin floor length dress with an overlay of three tiers of tulle. The bodice had narrow straps and pink-dyed embroidery appliqué hand sewn in a beautiful shape pattern. It was gorgeous.

As a second runner-up, Val was invited to compete at the nationals in California. We were so excited. My dear Scottish friend, upon hearing the good news, immediately donated money toward purchasing the necessary essentials. I began to prepare as the spirit led me. I made plans for her to do community volunteer service at the Goodwin House playing the piano for the elderly residents on Saturdays. This was one of the requirements for the pageant. I made her interview suit, filled out the forms, and made hotel reservations. The host hotel was all booked at the special rate for the pageant, but I was able to get a room for the first four nights only. I was trusting in the Lord because I knew that there might be cancellations as the pageant drew near. I had my name in their system and was given three days before the pageant to cancel my reservations.

I needed at least $2,000.00 to cover the pageant fees, entertainment, dinner, etc. One day, after praying, I heard the Holy Spirit said, "Have everything ready and leave it to me." I did everything necessary, except I hesitated to make her formal gown. It seemed that I prayed but still doubted that it was possible even though I heard loud and clear to "have everything ready."

I told myself that I could make the dress in two days, so I would wait until I mailed the package to the pageant committee. The rationale was, what if I made this formal gown and did not get the money? I still heard in my spirit to "get everything ready." I went to the UPS, made copies, got the large envelope, filled out and inserted the forms, and waited. Yet I did not obey. I did not purchase the materials to make the dress. Again, I was doubting God. What if? The deadline came, and there was still no money. Several deadline dates were given. Why could I not have taken God seriously and see what He was doing, especially when they had so many deadline dates. Yet I did not follow the instructions to make the dress.

What God wanted me to do was to trust Him completely. He said, "Have everything ready." That was the command. I did not do that one thing. I did not have everything ready. Now I know what I was supposed to do. When the Holy Spirit speaks, we must obey. I did not obey. I should have made the dress, had everything ready, and lifted them up to the Lord in obedience. I was given four deadline dates, and I missed out because of my disobedience. I failed. Like Moses, I asked God to forgive me for my lack of faith. The Bible tells us in Hebrews 11:1, "Faith is the substance of things hoped for the evidence of things not seen." I did not obey God, and we did not attend the pageant.

I had proven God in the past, and He did much greater things for me. Was it too hard for Him to have sent the money? The Bible tells us in Jeremiah 32:17 and 27, "Behold, I am the God of all flesh, is there anything too hard for me? Ah Lord God! Behold thou hast made the heaven and the earth by thy great power and stretched out arm, and there is nothing too hard for thee." In a split second, if only I had obeyed Him. The conviction I got after shedding so many tears. Like Moses, I said, "Forgive me, Lord, for my lack of faith." This is a lesson I would not forget as long as I live. I failed my granddaughter because of my disobedience. I hoped and prayed that the opportunity would again present itself.

Chapter 13

I was honored when both Sandra and Sonia asked me to make their wedding gowns. Susan, with a second marriage to a Chinese American, did not want me to make her wedding gown; she purchased a beautiful off-white silk satin knee-length dress. The ceremony and reception took place at the groom's aunt's home in Potomac, Maryland.

It was time to make Sandra's gown. It took two bolts of tulle netting for the skirt and veil. The bodice was made of beaded lace and a six-foot train. It was beautiful. Sandra married her Italian pen pal, who she met when we were on a cruise, and moved to Bassano del Grappa, Italy, where she taught English privately to students. It was my first trip to Italy when I visited the couple. I landed at Marco Polo Airport and was driven to Bassano del Grappa to their apartment. My son-in-law was my tour guide during my stay in Italy. I fell in love with Venice—this exotic city with landmarks such as the Basilica di San Marco. I was told it is one of Europe's most beautiful churches. We also visited the Palazzo Ducale, sumptuous palaces and romantic waterways—a beautiful masterpiece. We visited Piazza San Marco (St. Mark's Square) in the heart of Venice, filled with people and crowds of fluttering pigeons.

Next, we went on a visit to Murano, known for its glassworks, to see how glass, figurines, vases, and many interesting and beautiful things are made. A cruise down the canal and a walk over the Rialto Bridge to the surrounding markets were a wonderful experience. Next, we visited the Republic of San Marino. The winding road with sharp turns was a bit hair-raising. We drove about 9,000 feet up the Stelvio Pass. I was told it's the second highest pass in Europe. The view from the top was worth the effort; you could see Switzerland.

We drove through the Dolomite Mountains (The Italian Alps) and visited many other sites. We took a basket filled with food and found a perfect spot for a picnic, which was breathtaking. I kept praying for my son-in-law who had the task of driving, and he did an excellent job. Praise God. It was a wonderful experience.

All the time spent with my daughter, I did not know that she was pregnant, which accounted for her unusual behavior. One evening, I was reading my emails sent to me from my family, and suddenly, I felt ill and could not move because of the pain in my stomach. I asked my daughter if she could make me a cup of tea. The tea is ready, she said. I asked if she could bring it for me, and she said, "No, we do not eat or drink in the computer room, especially by the computer." I immediately got up, took the tea from the kitchen, and went to my room. No one came and asked how I was feeling, so I stayed there until the next morning, Oh well, that's life. Perhaps, being pregnant caused her to have those moods. I tried to tough it out and enjoy myself until it was time to leave.

When my first grandson was born, I took another trip to Italy. Alexander was born prematurely, and trips to the hospital twice a day were expected. He is his parents' pride and joy. Now he is a college graduate.

On the day of my departure, I encountered a very rude officer at the security gate. It was the most humiliating and embarrassing experience in all of my travels. At the Marco Polo Airport in Venice, I was about to pass through the metal detector when it went off. I was wearing an emerald green two-piece linen suit with a gemstone broach that might have triggered the detector. However, the young officer told me to take off my blouse so he could inspect it. I remembered my mother saying, "Always wear your very best when you are going out because you never know when something would happen to you." This is a joke I heard. A mother told her son to always put on clean underpants before leaving home. He got in an accident, and the first thing his mother asked him was "Did you have clean underpants on?" The officer told me to take off my blouse, displaying only my bra and skin. Then he said, "Okay, put your top on," and told me to go ahead.

Sandra wanted to return to the United States, but her husband did not have the proper papers to enter the country. After praying about the situation, I was inspired to write to my state senator, who took up the case and contacted the embassy in Italy, and God made a miraculous way for Sandra's husband to follow his wife.

After the engagement of Sonia, she decided to buy a single-family house with four bedrooms and three and a half baths. I continued to live with her and volunteered for four hours a week, which I enjoyed. When we moved into the family house, I asked the Lord to show me how I could make new friends in the neighborhood.

Now it was the time for Sonia to plan for her wedding. Making two wedding gowns, each a different style, was a challenge. Sonia's gown was a simple style, but it was very elegant. The dress had appliqué flowers with pearls and stones, which were hand sewn. It took me three months to finish the very detailed dress, and she wore a shoulder-length veil attached to a tiara.

The ceremony took place in Dahlgren Chapel on the campus of Georgetown University where she graduated. The elaborate reception was held at the Monarch Hotel in Washington DC. Sonia married her college mate in September 2001, two weeks after the 9/11 tragedy. They spent their honeymoon in Spain.

Chapter 14

After the wedding, things returned to normal. I became bored. Val would go to day care at Grandma B. With nothing else to do, I remembered receiving a flyer in the bottom of my mailbox to which I paid no attention to because I was on a mission to make a wedding gown. I picked up the flyer and read a letter from Patti, who lived in the neighborhood, inviting me to attend a women's prayer group meeting at her house. I immediately called and asked if I could attend. When I arrived at her home, I was introduced to thirteen friendly ladies. This is a ladies' prayer group, which meets every Tuesday morning at 9:30. First, we have breakfast, and then we study from the Bible. Each week, one person is responsible for bringing the meal and hosting the meeting.

After Patti and a few of the ladies moved from the area, we continued hosting at the various homes, but one of the ladies agreed to have the meeting at her home every Tuesday. It all began when Patti was putting the flyers in the mailboxes. She prayed and asked God to send at least one person to join the group. I was that one person.

Christmas is my favorite time of the year, and Thanksgiving is a time when I reflect on God's goodness to us when we had our first Thanksgiving in the United States of America. It is also a time when families get together to feast, to laugh, have conversations, play games, and do fun things. Most importantly, it is a time to give God thanks. I remembered the first Thanksgiving in the new single-family house. We were just about to serve dessert when suddenly, Susan's feathers got ruffled when she was asked not to pick up her dog at the table. I tried to say something to ease the tension. She got up out of her seat and came around by my chair, pushed me, and said, "You don't know who I am," and out came the swearing. Everyone was so stunned expecting me to get up and slap the hell out of her, but instead, I sat in my chair, too embarrassed to say anything. Finally, I got the nerve to ask her to leave, which she did with her husband, and a slew of curse words followed.

Her appearance at any other holiday affairs was certainly not my idea. It would have been at Sonia's invitation. That left a bitter taste in the family. To make matters worse, Sandra did not come to my defense. She said it was my fault because I should not have said what I said. I cannot remember what I said to deserve such disrespect.

I always wanted my independence. Living with my daughter and son-in-law is not what I had in mind. I enjoy having my grandchildren Val and Nick. When Nick was learning to talk, he would call me "Da." It sounded so sweet to hear him say "Da." Now they call me Grandy. I got the name Grandy from reading the book *Woman of Substance* by Barbara Taylor Bradford. It sounded so elegant that I thought my grandchildren should call me Grandy and not grandmother. Alexander, my first grandson, who lived about one and a half hours drive, didn't get to see me often. He only gets to see me on special occasions. I have asked his mother several times to allow him to spend a weekend or a day, but she refuses to unless she comes with him. Val is an A student; she also placed fourth in a Spelling Bee contest.

Chapter 15

O n November 27, 2010, I was travelling on 395 South heading home from volunteering at the airport. At around 6:00 p.m., I was driving in the right lane as I normally do after leaving the airport when I was hit on the passenger side by another car which apparently tried to pass me on the shoulder. The impact was so severe that I clutched the wheel with all my strength while the car kept spinning around. I believe it spun around about three or four times while I kept saying *"Jesus, Jesus, Jesus,* please help me." The car then came to a sudden stop against the guardrail. I thought I was going to die as I saw cars zooming by. After the car stopped and I realized what had happened, I called 911. Then I checked to see if I was bleeding or if any part of my body was damaged. My wig was still on my head. The State Troopers came, also an ambulance. I was not hurt, but the driver of the next car apparently was hurt because she was taken in the ambulance. She had no insurance and was given a ticket for speeding and reckless driving. At the hearing, the prosecutor asked me what punishment should be enforced—a fine of $500.00 or a more severe punishment? I was told that she was a foreign student. I said none of the above, just my deductible. She had to attend driving school and report to the court or else one of the above would be imposed on her.

Before the accident occurred, I had a dream that my car broke down on the street. I prayed, "God, I have no money to get another car. Please help me." One evening, I picked up my grandson from school, and the car sounded as if it was on its last leg. So I said to him, "Please pray for Grandy to get another car." God works in mysterious ways. I was able to purchase a good used car with the money I got from the insurance. The Bible tells us in Psalm 63:7, "Because thou hast been my help, therefore in the shadow of thy wings I will rejoice."

Susan accompanied me to the court, and while waiting for the case to be called, we were in the prosecutor's office lounge having a conversation. I said to my daughter, "One good thing that came out of this accident was I was able to purchase a car with the money I got from the insurance because the car was totaled." I remembered saying a prayer just a few days before the accident that I needed a car, but I didn't know where I would get the money. My daughter said something implying that I must have done something wrong that would have caused me to get in an accident (as though to say that I must have offended God). I was so hurt, but I said nothing. I just prayed in my heart for her.

I am very proud of my children's accomplishments, especially Sonia's. She is tenacious, brave, kind, and thoughtful among other things. One of her many qualities I admire the most is every Father's Day, I would receive a gift and a card from her saying "You are my father and mother." The little things she does, her love shines brightly. God placed her in my life for a time like this. She is my best friend and my confidant. I am proud to be her mother and father. God has worked so many miracles in my life, as you can see in the examples in the book. God loves you. Is God working miracles in your life? I hope this book teaches others to never let God out of your sight. Put Him first in everything you do and know that you are not done running God's race yet.

It is not how you begin. It is how you end. I am kissing my past goodbye. It is over. The problems of yesterday have no place in my life today. The Bible tells us in Jeremiah 29:11, "For I know the thoughts that I think toward you, said the Lord, thoughts of peace, and not evil, to give you an expected end."

I am excited about this new beginning in my life. God is faithful. He directed my steps and removed the scars. Life experiences prepares you for the future because you learn from your mistakes. Experience, to me, is like pruning your garden or a tree to see new growth. When things happen that you don't understand, and it makes no sense, just know that God is pruning. He is directing your steps for new growth so you can experience more fruits in your life. Everything is God's plan. I chose to move forward in faith to victory as I focus on God's promise. The Bible tells us in Isaiah 43:19, "Behold, I will do a new thing, now shall spring forth; I will make a way in the wilderness, and rivers in the desert." Every dream and every promise, God has fulfilled. I could be one of God's end-time millionaires. The Bible tells us in Proverbs 10:22, "The blessing of the Lord, it maketh rich, and He addeth no sorrow with it."

When I heard of the passing of my husband from the members of my family, I was not saddened by the news. Now I know that he cannot hurt me anymore. Memories came flashing before my eyes, and I immediately cast them aside and buried them in a hole.

I am free. I can sing "Hallelujah! I have won the victory."

"Hallelujah! I have won the lottery."

Amen.

The Bible tells us:

> I waited patiently for the Lord, and He inclined unto me. And heard my cry. He brought me up also out of a horrible pit, out of the miry clay, and set my feet upon a rock, and established my goings. He put a new song in my mouth, even praise unto my God: many shall see it, and fear, and trust in the Lord (Psalm 40:1–2).

Healings

There were several times that God, through Jesus Christ, healed me; but I prefer to make mention of just a few. I remembered something disturbed me greatly, which caused a lump to settle in my throat. I did everything I could, but it would not go away. It kept getting bigger and bigger. I requested prayers at the Oral Roberts Prayer Tower. After a few weeks and nothing happened, I continued to trust God for His healing. As I laid in my bed asleep on a Saturday night, when it was around 2:00 a.m., I stirred and laid on my back, and I remembered saying, "God, please heal me." Just as I dozed off with my mouth slightly parted, I felt a cool breeze across my face and into my mouth. I woke up and the lump was gone. I was completely healed. I could not sleep anymore. Instead, I kept praising God and feeling my throat. That Sunday morning, I was looking at the Oral Roberts healing service on the television, and Oral announced that someone got a healing in their throat. I claimed that healing and praised God.

Healing Touch

I attended a revival and healing service in Crystal City at the Holiday Crown Hotel where the Rev. Peter Popoff was conducting a service. I sat in the second row praying for my healing to begin that night. Something had me clawing at my throat. It was so awful looking. When I arrived at the service, I had to tie a scarf around my throat, but when the service began, I removed the scarf. During the service, Reverend Popoff came and touched me and said, "The Holy Spirit wants to anoint your throat from cancer." That was history. I came away praising and thanking God for my healing because Reverend Popoff said my skin would return to normal like a little child. Praise God, I am healed. Praise God.

One morning, I woke up and looked in the mirror to see my face almost as white as a sheet and the skin as hard as parchment paper, without any warning, not even an itch. I made an appointment to see a doctor. After several tests, I was referred to a dermatologist. After two hospital visits for skin tests and over $3,000 in bills, no one seemed to understand the nature of what they saw. I would actually claw at my face with my nails. I was afraid to look into the mirror. I knew it was an evil attack.

I looked like I was a leprosy victim, but I kept on praying. Then one night, I woke up at around 2:00 a.m. and went in my prayer closet to pray before going back to bed. That night, something unusual happened. Just as I was entering the closet half asleep, I heard a very clear voice saying "Don't put your hands on your face." Then the voice told me what to do. I heard: I am the God that healeth thee. I knelt down and praised God for His healing, did what He told me to do, and went back to bed. About three days later, my face was back to normal and my skin was clear like that of a baby. I am praising God more every day of my life. *Praise God. Thank you, Jesus, for healing me.*

CPSIA information can be obtained
at www.ICGtesting.com
Printed in the USA
BVHW071540020223
657731BV00006B/159